Contents

KV-241-116

Core assignments

Focus assignments

Information pages

Introduction

This series is designed to help students meet the criteria laid down by the Joint Board for the new Certificate of Pre-Vocational Education. It aims to fulfil the three main requirements of CPVE courses:

(a) the integration of a core of basic skills with a wide-ranging choice of vocational studies;
(b) activity-based learning; and
(c) a flexibility that enables courses to be tailored to the needs of individual students.

The books in the series are arranged in two groups: one group concentrates on developing the main core competences, using different vocational settings; the other concentrates on the skills required in the vocational categories (the CPVE introductory and exploratory modules), but also provide practice in the core competences.

Each book consists of twenty assignments which develop skills in both general and specific vocational contexts. Ten of these concentrate on skills in general vocational contexts and ten on specific vocational situations (see diagram).

Main core competences	Core Skills in Communication	Core Skills in Numeracy	Core Skills in Industrial, Social and Environmental Studies	Core Skills in Science and Technology	Core Skills in Information Technology
	10 Core assignments (general vocational contexts) 10 Focus assignments (specific vocational situations) 10 Information pages				

Course

	10 Introductory assignments (general vocational contexts) 10 Exploratory assignments (specific vocational situations) 10 Information pages						
Vocational skills	Core Skills in Business and Administrative Services	Core Skills in Information Technology and Micro-electronic Systems	Core Skills in Service Engineering	Core Skills in Manufacture	Core Skills in Craft-based Activities	Core Skills in Distribution	Core Skills in Services to People

£3·95

The Macmillan Pre-Vocational Series

Core Skills in Communication

Judith Irving and Norman Smith

COLLEGE LIBRARY
COLLEGE OF TECHNOLOGY
CARNARVON ROAD
SOUTHEND-ON-SEA. ESSEX

IRVING, JUDITH
CORE SKILLS IN COMMUNICATION.
JUDITH IRVING AND NORMAN SMITH
302. 2   38-587591

30130503959116

Macmillan Education

Acknowledgments

The author and publishers wish to acknowledge the following sources:

AA Legal Services p 95; British Aircraft Corporation p 22; Bond Securities p 20; Camera Press Ltd pp 33, 39; Cosmopolitan p 16 (r); Debenhams Ltd p 20; DHSS p 116; Lloyds Bank Plc p 20; London Transport p 42; Rally Sports Magazine p 16 (1); Sealink UK Ltd p 9; Taylor Richardson Associates p 57; Vauxhall Motors Ltd p 71.

The publishers have made every effort to trace the copyright holders, but if they have inadvertently overlooked any, they will be pleased to make the necessary arrangements at the first opportunity.

The authors would also like to thank the following people: the library staff of Bournemouth and Poole College of Further Education, especially Rosemary Beale for her help with both 'Penfield Film Club' and 'Selling spree'; Robert Cowdrey of the Motor Vehicle Division for his suggestions concerning 'Selling spree'; and David Mason JP and the staff of Poole Magistrates Court for their invaluable assistance with 'The law decides'. We would also like to thank Andrea Etherington, Anne Corbin, Judith Edgley, Steven White, John Roberts and Malcolm Butcher of the Poole Social Studies Unit, for their help in using and analysing some of the assignments; not forgetting our students for their forbearance in acting as guinea pigs!

This book is dedicated to the memory of John and Elizabeth Smith and to the memory of Ruth Ingelfield

© Judith Irving and Norman Smith 1986

All rights reserved. No reproduction, copy or transmission
of this publication may be made without written permission.

No paragraph of this publication may be reproduced, copied
or transmitted save with written permission or in accordance
with the provisions of the Copyright Act 1956 (as amended).

Any person who does any unauthorised act in relation to
this publication may be liable to criminal prosecution and
civil claims for damages.

First published 1986

ESSEX COUNTY LIBRARY

Published by
MACMILLAN EDUCATION LTD
Houndmills, Basingstoke, Hampshire RG21 2XS and London
Companies and representatives throughout the world

Typeset by Wessex Typesetters
Frome, Somerset

Printed in Great Britain by Vine & Gorfin Ltd., Exmouth, Devon

British Library Cataloguing in Publication Data
Irving, Judith
Core skills in communication.—(The Macmillan
pre-vocational series)
1. Communication—Great Britain 2. Youth—
Great Britain—Life skills guides
I. Title II. Smith, Norman III. Series
302.2 P92.G7
ISBN 0–333–38837–2

X CK56341

0001251 IRV

The assignments are free-standing and can be combined in different modular ways according to individual course needs. To assist selection and combination, the objectives of each assignment are given both at its head and in a grid at the beginning of each book. At the end of each book information pages give facts and advice to support the activities in the assignments.

Core Skills in Communication has ten core assignments set in contexts familiar to students. They involve listening, speaking, reading and writing, and organising, interpreting and conveying information. The ten focus assignments apply these skills to concrete vocational situations, such as deciding where to site new industrial plant or selecting new residents for an old people's home. Ten information pages provide guidance on key activities such as report writing, note making, public speaking, and memoranda.

The material in this volume is also suitable for a wide range of other communication teaching, such as in: YTS off-the-job training; National Certificate (Scotland); RSA Vocational Preparation courses; City and Guilds (772) Certificate in Communication Skills; AEB Test in Basic English; and developing BTEC courses.

CPVE grid

Assignments	1.1	1.2	2.1	2.2	2.3	2.4	2.5	3.1	3.2	3.3	4.1	4.2	5.1	5.2	5.3	5.4	5.5	5.6	5.7	5.8	5.9	5.10	5.11	5.12
1 Ban education cuts				■		■		■		■				■				■						
2 Penfield Pharmaceuticals takes a trip	■	■	■	■	■	■	■		■	■	■	■	■		■	■	■	■	■	■	■	■		
3 Questioning unemployment	■	■	■	■	■	■	■	■	■	■	■	■	■	■		■	■	■	■	■	■	■		
4 Mass media	■	■	■	■	■	■	■	■	■	■	■	■	■	■	■	■	■	■	■		■		■	■
5 Talking about finance	■	■	■	■		■	■	■	■	■	■	■	■	■	■	■	■	■	■	■				
6 New technology?	■	■	■	■	■	■	■	■	■	■	■	■	■	■	■	■	■	■	■					
7 Problem page	■	■	■	■	■	■	■	■		■		■	■		■	■		■	■					
8 Penfield Film Club	■	■	■	■	■	■	■	■	■	■	■		■		■	■		■	■					
9 Sponsored fun	■	■	■	■	■	■	■	■		■	■	■	■	■	■	■	■		■					
10 The law decides	■	■	■	■	■	■	■	■	■	■	■	■	■	■	■	■	■	■	■					
11 Lytchett Engineering plc	■	■	■	■	■	■	■	■	■	■	■	■	■	■	■	■	■	■		■		■		
12 New site for Olds	■	■	■	■	■	■	■	■	■	■	■	■	■	■	■	■	■	■	■					
13 Colourful club	■	■	■	■	■	■	■	■		■	■		■		■	■	■	■						
14 Redevelopment	■	■	■	■	■	■	■	■	■		■	■	■	■	■	■	■	■						
15 Treasure hunt	■	■	■	■	■	■	■	■	■	■	■	■	■	■	■	■	■	■	■				■	
16 Motoring choice	■	■	■	■	■	■	■	■	■	■	■	■	■	■	■	■	■	■	■					
17 Brookdale Old People's Home	■	■	■	■	■	■	■	■	■	■	■	■	■	■	■	■	■	■	■					
18 Catering for Christmas	■	■	■	■	■	■	■	■		■	■	■	■	■	■	■	■	■		■		■		
19 Charity can be profitable	■	■	■	■	■	■	■	■	■	■	■	■	■	■	■	■	■	■	■				■	
20 Selling spree	■	■	■	■	■	■	■	■	■	■	■	■	■	■	■	■	■		■					

Core assignments

1 Ban education cuts

AIM

To develop your written and graphic skills in
- presenting information
- expressing facts and information in a persuasive manner

Introduction

The local education authority is threatening to make financial cuts in education, which could mean that there would be fewer students able to undertake full-time courses and would, in some instances, mean that certain students would not be eligible for a grant. The authority is also threatening to make cuts in some full-time courses, as well as those run for day-release students.

There is to be a student rally held in London soon, starting with a march from Trafalgar Square to the Houses of Parliament, where students will lobby their own MPs.

Your student union wants to send as many students as possible to represent the establishment, and in order to promote interest in the event it has asked students to design posters advertising the forthcoming rally. These will be displayed in the institution.

Task 1

As a member of the student union, you have agreed to design a poster advertising the forthcoming rally in London. Your poster should aim to be persuasive, but it should also contain basic information about the rally and why you feel this is a worthy cause to support.

You have also been asked to think of a catchy and punchy slogan that could be adopted by students and used on badges and banners at the rally. Assume that the rally will be held in five weeks' time.

Task 2

As a group (the Student Union Committee) your task is to meet and choose one of the poster and slogan entries to be used in your forthcoming campaign.

The Committee also has to decide how representation at the rally will be organised. For example, will it be official, with transport provided, or unofficial, leaving students to find their own way to the rally?

Task 3

Figure 1 contains three letters that have recently appeared in the *Penfield Telegraph*, agreeing with local education authority proposals for financial cuts in education. You feel so strongly about these letters that you decide to write to the editor, putting forward your own viewpoint. You need only reply to *one* of these letters.

IMPORTANT

Read this information page:
A Committee meetings

Figure 1   Extracts from a local newspaper

Penfield Telegraph

EDITOR'S POST BAG

'TOO EASY FOR YOUNG PEOPLE'

SIR – There has been considerable publicity in the newspapers recently about the proposed cuts in education, and I am amazed to learn that our own local schools and colleges are proposing to send students to demonstrate against these cuts at the forthcoming student rally to be held in London.

I personally feel that too much money is spent on education these days and that the young people don't really appreciate it. What with all these elaborate schemes they keep thinking of such as YOPS and YTS and lots of other fancy names when half the time they can't even fill the places because the youngsters would rather draw dole money than have to go to college and do something useful for the money they are getting from the state.

I had to leave school at fourteen years of age and get a job in an engineering factory and go to night school. There was none of this nonsense about being offered a day off a week to study at college or get a grant, let alone being given the opportunity to go to school or college for another two years of full-time study.

I am a grandfather with two teenage grandchildren and I want to see them get on in the world, but I feel that we make things too easy for the young people of today.

So I say well done to the local councillors in trying to make these cuts, and perhaps some of the money they save could be spent on giving the old-age pensioners of this area some better community facilities to help them enjoy their well-deserved retirement. – BILL GRAHAM, OAP (address supplied)

'MORE MONEY FOR NURSERY EDUCATION'

SIR – I am a single parent with two children, aged seven years and three years of age respectively, and I would like to support the local council in the attempts they are making to curb spending in the fields of further and higher education.

I feel there is already sufficient provision made in this section of education whilst other areas are suffering quite severely and have been for many years, particularly in the area of statutory educational provision for the under-fives.

I was recently offered a well-paid part-time job as a health visitor, which is what I used to be before I had my children. I have had to turn this job down because I have been unable to obtain a place at nursery school for my three-year-old daughter.

It appears there is only one nursery school run by the local Education Authority in this town, and that in order for your child to qualify for a place, you have to have family problems or be a child batterer, because when I tried to obtain a place for my daughter I was told that the application would have to be made through the local Social Services Department, who would then decide on my daughter's eligibility for a place.

This seems quite ludicrous to me, when I actually *WANT* to work and not be dependent on supplementary benefit. Therefore I feel that the Local Authority should go ahead with their plans to make cuts in the area of further and higher education but *PLEASE PLEASE* channel some of the money into nursery education for the under-fives because many single parents *ACTUALLY WANT TO GO TO WORK AND CANNOT.* – MS. PAULA YOUNG, SCM SRN HV's Cert. (address supplied)

'DECLINING STANDARDS'

SIR – I am an ordinary resident who lives close to Penfield High School and I felt I had to write and express my views when I learnt that young people from the school propose attending a rally in London shortly to demonstrate against the education cuts which our Local Authority and others propose to make.

All I can say is that if the young people I see going in and out of school each day represent the average school population of today, then I shouldn't think any government in their right mind would take any notice of them!!!

I mean they have all sorts of hairstyles, including spikes with pink and blue streaks, and none of them seem to care what they wear so it just seems that anything goes these days. They wear earrings in one ear and that's boys as well as girls. They go into school kissing and cuddling and entwined around one another. No one seems to stop them or care.

And as for the teachers, well to be frank, as far as I can see they certainly don't set the young people any kind of example because half of them are just as sloppily dressed.

I feel that our moral as well as social standards are declining and unless people in positions of authority such as lecturers, teachers, social workers, youth workers and the police take stock and do something about it things are going to go from bad to worse but I certainly don't feel that any government in its right mind will take notice of the sort of young people who will attend this rally in London. – ERNIE THOMAS (address supplied)

2 Penfield Pharmaceuticals takes a trip

AIM

To develop your skills in
- obtaining information from a variety of sources
- making considered choices

Introduction

This assignment involves you, as a committee member of Penfield Pharmaceuticals' Social Club, in organising an outing for the members of that club. Not only will you have to help choose a suitable outing, but you will also be involved in researching and estimating its cost.

At a previous meeting, the committee decided that it might be a good idea to organise a day trip for Social Club members. A meeting has been called to discuss this issue. Before starting any of the tasks, examine Figures 1 and 2.

Task 1

You meet as the Social Club Committee, remembering to select a chairperson before beginning your meeting. As part of the agenda your committee has the task of choosing three possible places to visit on your day out. Your first task, as a group, is to select three possible trips.

You will find it helpful to jot down notes during the meeting (for use in Task 2). We have included, in Figure 3, a selection of ideas for possible outings, but you are free to use your own ideas.

Task 2

The committee has decided that to help choose between these three possible outings, small working groups should be set up to examine, in detail, the itinerary and estimated cost of each outing.

The chairperson has divided the group into three sub-groups: each sub-group will look at one proposal in detail and produce a written, informal report. The chairperson should join one of the three sub-groups.

Each sub-group should estimate the total cost of the trip, and should also indicate in its report how the trip would be financed. For example, should the outing be totally self-financing, or should some or all of the cost be met from Social Club funds? If the outing is to be self-financing, then the report should indicate the cost per person of the outing.

Figure 4 gives an analysis of the Club's present financial position. You should note carefully the financial standing of the Club at present and remember that the Club is not allowed to run with a financial deficit.

You may use the library and other facilities to find out the true cost of your proposed outing. For example, you might want to telephone a local coach company for an estimate of the cost of hiring a coach or minibus for a day.

Task 3

The committee now meets to decide on the best proposal for an outing. Before any discussion takes place about the choice of outing, members of each sub-group should verbally present their ideas. In reaching its final decision, the committee should consider not only financial matters but the likely appeal of the proposed outings.

____ **IMPORTANT** ____

Read these information pages:
A Committee meetings
B Report writing

Figure 1   Extract from a leaflet

A brief history of Penfield Pharmaceuticals' Social Club

Penfield Pharmaceuticals plc began trading in the early 1960s. It is situated on a trading estate on the outskirts of Penfield. The firm has 250 staff, 170 of whom are women.

The Social Club was started five years ago with only 20 members. However, each year it has continued to expand and at present has a membership of 183 people.

The present subscription rate is £5.00 per annum, and the firm itself provides the Club with a further £5.00 for each member.

Last year the committee spent most of its money on subscriptions to various local sports leagues and the firm was represented at such sporting activities as football, badminton, darts, tennis and keep-fit.

At the Annual General Meeting earlier in the year, it was decided to continue the policy of sponsoring sporting activities, and also to encourage new membership from the non-sporting fraternity by organising such things as outings, skittles evenings, and an annual dinner and dance.

At the moment the Club has no buildings of its own and meets in the firm's canteen.

Figure 2 Extract from a leaflet

The constitution and rules of Penfield Pharmaceuticals' Social Club

A Title

1 The organisation shall be called, 'The Penfield Pharmaceuticals' Social Club' (hereafter referred to as 'the Club').

B Aims and objectives

1 The aims and objectives of the Club shall be the furtherance of social activities among colleagues working for Penfield Pharmaceuticals; and where possible the aiding, by financial means, of local charities.

C Subscriptions

1 The membership subscription for the ensuing year shall be fixed annually at the Annual General Meeting of the Club.
2 Prospective members may participate in one meeting of one activity without payment; thereafter a charge will be made, this charge being fixed at the Annual General Meeting.
3 The Club's financial year shall run from 1 February to 31 January and all subscriptions shall be due on 1 May each year.
4 The Club shall be conducted on a non-profit-making basis. Any surplus at the end of any financial year shall be donated to charity and any long-term projects on a 50/50 basis.
5 The Club's income shall be devoted to general expenses in running the Club and to charity: no payment for any services shall be made to any member.
6 Any equipment purchased from Club funds shall be considered part of the assets of the Club.
7 Any activity defined beforehand as a charity event is allowed to recoup its costs only. All profits must go to charity.

D Management

1 The management of the Club shall be in the hands of a Committee consisting of six elected members.
2 These Committee members shall be elected annually from the Club's membership and they shall be elected at the Annual General Meeting.
3 The Committee will itself elect a Chairperson, a Secretary and a Treasurer.
4 The Committee shall have the power to co-opt any member with specialised knowledge, as it thinks fit.
5 No co-opted member has voting rights.
6 The quorum for a committee meeting shall be three members.

E   General meetings

1   A General Meeting of the Club shall be held annually in the month of June and fourteen days' notice of the meeting shall be given to members, in writing, with the agenda of the meeting and details of the resolutions to be discussed.
2   A Special General Meeting may be called by the Committee at any time, and shall be called on written request being made to the Secretary, by a minimum of one-third of the membership.
3   Fourteen days' notice in writing shall be given of any Special General Meeting, together with details of the resolutions to be discussed.
4   The quorum for a General Meeting of the Club shall be one-fifth of the membership.

F   Expulsion

1   The Committee shall have the power to expel any member who offends against the rules of the Club, or whose conduct has, in the opinion of the Committee, rendered such a member unfit for membership.
2   The member concerned shall have the right to attend the committee meeting at which the expulsion is to be discussed, and seven days' notice that such a meeting is to be held shall be given.

Figure 3   Some suggestions for possible Social Club outings

Day trips
- London, to see the sights or go shopping
- France, to visit a hypermarket and to have a French meal
- the seaside
- a historic house
- a wildlife park
- a famous garden
- a pottery or glassworks
- a river or canal trip
- a mystery tour

Figure 4   Extract from a balance sheet

Analysis of the current financial position

Income		*Expenditure*	
Membership fees		Subscriptions to	
(£5.00 per member)	£ 915.00	various sports leagues	£ 455.00
Subsidy from		Annual Christmas	
management	£ 915.00	party for OAPs	£ 245.00
Fund-raising dance		Annual Christmas	
(Self-financing)	£ 36.25	party for employees'	
Donations	£ 15.30	children	£ 200.00
		Day trip to Isle of	
		Wight (80 people;	
		50% self-financing)	£ 265.96
		To local hospital's	
		body-scanner appeal	£ 250.00
TOTAL	£1881.55	*TOTAL*	£1415.96
		Present income	£1881.55
		Present expenditure	£1415.96
		BALANCE	+£ 465.59

3
Questioning unemployment

_____ **AIM** _____
To develop your skills in
- formulating questionnaires
- analysing the advantages and limitations of questionnaires
- presenting information in a statistical format

Introduction
This assignment is centred on a survey based on a questionnaire.

A local newspaper has asked a small group of students to conduct a survey on youth unemployment. The newspaper specifically wants to find out what students feel about:

(a) the causes of unemployment;
(b) how groups of unemployed young people could best occupy their time; and
(c) what such groups as students' unions should be doing to help them.

Your task is to produce a questionnaire and to carry out a survey that will get the answers to the questions posed above in such a form that you will be able to analyse the results statistically.

Task 1
Prepare a draft questionnaire, consisting of approximately 12–15 questions, which will aim to answer the three questions posed by the newspaper.

Task 2
Once your questionnaire has been formulated and tested you can conduct your survey. Ideally this should involve about one hundred participants. Make sure that your participants represent a rough cross-section of the local community.

Task 3
As a group, you now have to analyse the answers you received to your questions. When doing this you should bear in mind that the answers are to be presented in statistical format.

Task 4
The group has given you the task of presenting the results as statistical data. It is up to you to decide which is the best way of presenting them.

____ **IMPORTANT** ____
Read these information pages:
C Social-survey techniques
D Compiling and presenting statistics

Unemployment Reaches
3 Million

SCHOOL LEAVERS FACE THE DOLE

---

4 Mass media

AIM

To develop your skills in
● using communication
  techniques to present
  information and ideas

Introduction

You have decided, as a small group (approximately six in a group), that student life has become rather routine and boring lately and that you would like to try and brighten it up. You have had the idea of producing a termly student magazine in a written format, or – if this is not possible – a termly student magazine programme that could be broadcast to students via the Student Union closed-circuit television and loudspeaker facilities in college, or on the library video or tape recorders.

You have been advised that before you can proceed with the idea, you must seek the Principal's agreement. Therefore your first task is as follows:

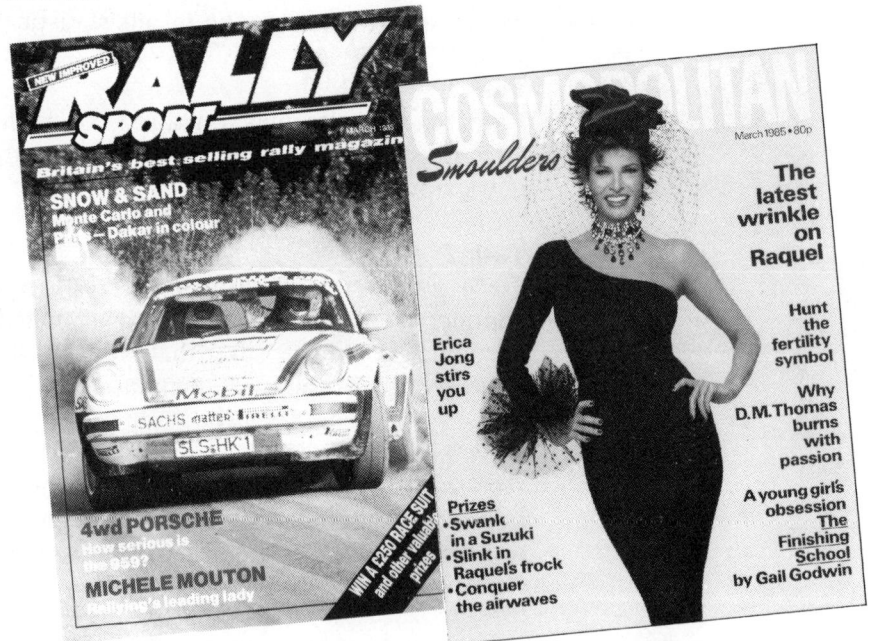

Task 1

As a group you must write a memo to the Principal, setting out your idea for a college magazine or magazine programme, and explaining why you think this would be a good idea and also how you would wish to use college facilities (such as reprographics or video-tape and sound-tape editing equipment).

Remember that the aim of your memo is to get the Principal's agreement, so the tone of the memo will need to be persuasive.

Task 2

You can assume that the Principal has given his or her permission for the idea to go ahead. You now have to meet together as a group to decide what kind of format your magazine will take. You have three choices:
(a) a written magazine;
(b) a fifteen-minute radio programme; or
(c) a fifteen-minute television programme.
Note that the format you decide upon for your magazine will affect the amount, content and presentation of material used.

Task 3

Now you have decided on the format your magazine is going to take, you must consider what material to use. This is going to be a first edition, so you must aim to make it popular and interesting in order to convince both staff and students that your magazine should become an ongoing part of student life. You will need to make your topic ideas relevant and interesting to your audience.

Figure 1 contains some suggestions for possible topic areas. *These are only suggestions* and you are free to include ideas of your own. Bear in mind that you will need to produce more material than you think you will need, so that you can edit it.

Task 4

Having decided on the items that you are going to include in your magazine, gather together the necessary information for each item. Remember that you are working as a group, so you will have to decide who is going to gather information for each particular item, and who is going to be in overall charge of the group. You will also need to decide whether items for inclusion should be individual ones or compiled as a group. Once you have gathered your information together, it will be necessary to adapt it to the format of the presentation you have chosen.

Task 5

Prepare a final draft of your magazine or magazine programme so that you can assess:
(a) a suitable title;
(b) the layout or order of presentation of information; and
(c) the style of presentation.

___ **IMPORTANT** ___

Read these information pages:
A Committee meetings
D Compiling and
   presenting statistics
E Writing articles
F Note making
G Public speaking

If you have sufficient time, you may find it interesting and rewarding to go on and either to write up the magazine or to record on video-tape or audio-tape the magazine programme you have prepared. You can then compare your presentation with that of other groups.

Remember that decisions have to be made about what is and what is not to be included in your magazine. This can be done either by using an 'editorial board' involving all students in the group, or by giving the responsibility to one group member as editor.

Figure 1   Some suggested topics

Budgeting on a low income
Borrowing money
Young people and the police
Bed-sitter cookery
Video review
Drugs and young people
Leaving home for the first time
Contraception
State benefits for the young
Record review
Abortion – pros and cons
Weekend and holiday jobs
Smoking and public health
Making the most of unemployment
This week's TV or radio for the student viewer/listener
Opening a bank account
The problems of being self-employed
Renting a flat or bed-sitter
Hitch-hiking
Disco dancing
Film review
Holidays on a limited budget
What's happening in your area?

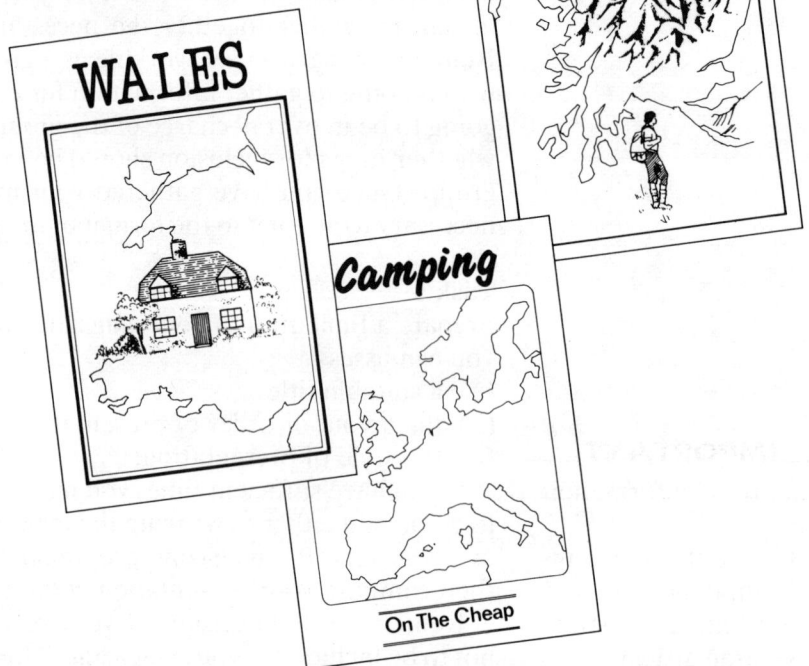

Adventure Vacations

WALES

Camping

On The Cheap

5 Talking about finance

Talking about finance

AIM

To develop your oral skills in
- formally presenting information

Introduction

This assignment is a public-speaking exercise. Your aim is to prepare a five-minute *illustrated* talk on an aspect of finance, and then to present it to your colleagues.

Task 1

You first have to choose the topic on which you are going to talk.

Figure 1 (on page 20) contains a list of some likely topics. This is only a suggested list: you can choose any other topic that you prefer.

Before moving to Task 2, check your choice with your tutor.

Task 2

Your task is to prepare, using various sources of information, a set of notes on your chosen topic.

Task 3

This task involves two activities:
(a) selecting the information that you are going to give your audience (remember that you only have five minutes); and
(b) selecting those areas of your talk in which illustrations will be used.

Task 4

Prepare your illustrations.

Task 5

Prepare your talk, on cards or separate sheets.

Task 6

Present your talk to your colleagues.

IMPORTANT

Read these information pages:
F Note making
G Public speaking

Figure 1   Some suggested topic areas

Here is a list of possible topics, which might stimulate ideas for a talk on finance.

The history of British banking
The Bank of England
Banks and industry
Banks and the individual
Banking services

Finance houses
Hire purchase
Obtaining credit facilities
Types of borrowing
Finance and unemployment

Social-security benefits
Finance and setting up a business
Building societies
Post Office savings
Investing money
The Stock Exchange

Insurance
Foreign currencies
History of money
Income tax
National Insurance

Value-Added Tax
Running a car
Getting married
Inflation
Old-age pensions

Credit facilities take many different forms

DEBENHAMS

the CHARGE CARD

Debenhams
CHARGE CARD
759 40 168
SUSAN JAMES
SERIES 2

for all your shopping

BOND SECURITIES
LOANS
AT GENUINE LOW INTEREST RATES
£1,000 - £50,000 (3-25 years).
CASH FOR ANY PURPOSE
Compare our repayment costs with ANY other Leading Broker.
IMMEDIATE DECISIONS MADE.
TELEPHONE 0203 52102 (6 lines)
BOND SECURITIES
Sovereign House 16a Queens Rd., Coventry, West Midlands CV1 3EG

Rates of interest
until further notice
Lloyds Bank
A thoroughbred amongst banks

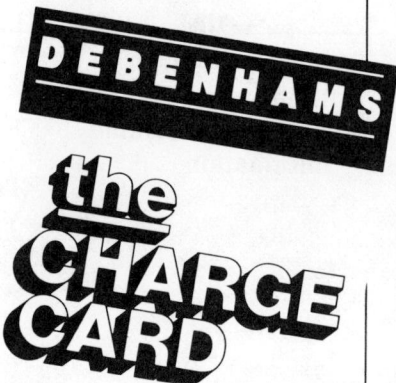

6 New technology?

_____ **AIM** _____

To develop your skills in
- collecting and analysing information and data
- presenting the results to an audience using effective communication techniques

Introduction

In the latest editions of the local newspaper, various people have expressed opinions about recent scientific and technological developments (see Figure 1). You have decided that it would be worthwhile for a small group to conduct a survey on one of these subject areas, to assess how much people are aware of what is going on in this particular field. Once the survey has been completed, you will analyse the questionnaires and note the specific areas with which people are unfamiliar.

You will then have to decide what would be the most effective way of filling this knowledge gap. You must decide how you can communicate information about your topic area, quickly and efficiently, to as large an audience as possible.

Task 1
Read Figure 1, which is a list of suggested topic areas. You may use one of them, or you may prefer to think of your own ideas. Your first task, as a small group, is to decide on one topic area on which to base your survey.

Task 2
Once you have decided on a particular topic, devise a questionnaire that will achieve the aims set out in the introduction to this assignment. To devise meaningful questions you will need to be informed about the topic that you have chosen to investigate.

Task 3
After you have compiled your questionnaire, test it out on a few people to see if it achieves the required objectives. Then conduct your survey. You should aim to interview at least fifty people, making sure that your survey is representative of both sexes and an appropriate range of ages.

Task 4
Analyse the results of your survey. It will be necessary to present these results in statistical format, as you will need this analysis to help you complete Task 5.

Task 5
As a group, you must now decide:
(a) what areas people are unfamiliar with; and

(b) what will be the most effective method of informing people about these areas.

_____IMPORTANT_____

Read these information pages:
C Social-survey techniques
D Compiling and presenting statistics
E Writing articles

Task 6

As a group it is now your task to carry out the decision reached in Task 5b. For example, you may have decided that the most effective method of informing people is to produce a short video programme, or you may have decided that it would be more effective to write an article for the local newspaper. Remember that the choice is yours, but the main aim is to inform people about your group's topic and to inform as many people as possible using the most effective methods.

Figure 1   Some suggested topic areas

Here is a list of topic areas for use in conjunction with this assignment. Groups should only choose one topic area. Remember that you are free to use your own ideas.

Nuclear energy
Electronic money
Electronic mail
Robots in industry
Genetic engineering
Electronic news-gathering
Satellite communication
Computers in the home
Developments in space
Biochemistry – scientific food production
Future trends in the use of computers and microprocessors
Synthetic music

A communications satellite

7 Problem page

AIM

To develop your written and graphic skills in
- organising and editing written material
- expressing views in a sympathetic and constructive manner

Dear Maggie **PROBLEM PAGE** *Dear Tony*
COMING SOON!
NEW 'READERS' PROBLEMS' FEATURE FOR YOUR MAGAZINE
ANYONE WITH PROBLEMS SHOULD WRITE NOW!
SHARE YOUR PROBLEMS WITH MAGGIE AND TONY, CARE OF THE STUDENT UNION OFFICE

Introduction

This advertisement appeared in the last edition of your monthly college magazine, inviting students with problems to write in for advice.

As a member of the magazine's editorial board you have been given the job of designing and developing this new feature for the college magazine. You and a small group of other students will be responsible for replying to letters and preparing the problem page for publication.

Task 1

Your first task is to meet as an editorial board and to decide what is the most appropriate advice, in general terms, to give to each of the people who have written in (see Figure 1). You will find it helpful to take brief notes during this task.

Task 2

Using the notes that you prepared in Task 1, compose suitable personal replies to *two* of the letters.

Task 3

The magazine can only afford to devote one A4 page to this new venture until it is clear that it is going to be a success. As the member of the editorial committee with overall responsibility for this page, you have to decide:
(a) how many letters you are going to include, bearing in mind that you will have to leave space for the replies;
(b) whether you will edit the letters or leave them complete; and
(c) a title for the new feature, and appropriate headings for each of the included letters.

____IMPORTANT____

Read these information
pages:
A Committee meetings
F Note making

Task 4

You are now ready to produce a draft layout of the problem page for
approval by the editor. This draft should indicate where the letters and
their replies will be situated on the page. You should also write out
appropriate headings for each of the letters, and the title of the whole
feature. Remember that it is important to preserve confidentiality.

**Figure 1   Letters received by the Students' Union for their new
problem page**

Letter 1

> Dear Tony,
>
>   I was recently invited to a party and normally
> I won't go because I hate parties. I would rather
> stay at home or just go out with one friend but I
> was talked into it and had the most miserable
> time.
>
>   I just find it impossible to talk to people and
> when people come up to me and start up a conversation
> I just feel tongue tied and go red. I feel as if the
> words won't come out and that I can't think — it's
> even worse when I try to talk to a girl.
>
>   Fortuately it was dark so I don't think anyone
> saw how embarrassed I was but I spent most of
> the evening hiding in the kitchen and left early
> because I couldn't face it any longer.
>
>   Other young people just don't seem to suffer
> from the same problem. I am eighteen now and things
> aren't getting any better, so please what can I do?
> My social life is a misery.
>
>   Paul.

Letter 2

> Dear Maggie
>   My boyfriend works in a garage as a motor
> mechanic and even in his spare time he is always
> tinkering with cars. In fact his dad makes him
> even worse because he is interested in doing
> up old cars as well.
>
>   The problem is that he always has dirty,
> greasy hands, the grease is embedded all
> around his nails and to make matters even
> worse he bites them. This isn't even the
> worst of his problems, I'm afraid he isn't
> too particular about his personal hygiene. In
> fact to put it plainly it isn't pleasant to
> be near him sometimes.
>
>   He has a really nice personality and I don't
> want to end our relationship but how
> can I tell him about these problems
> without hurting his feelings?

Letter 3

Dear Maggie & Tony

I am in the second year of a full time 'A' level course at college and I hope to be able to go on to polytechnic or university to study for a degree in mechanical engineering, but I am finding the situation at home almost intolerable at the moment.

There are continual arguments between myself and my mother. I just can't seem to do anything right whether it's my clothes, my friends or the time that I come home at night. I have a younger fourteen year old brother and he can't seem to do anything wrong. I have tried to talk to my father about the problem but he always seems to take my mother's side. The arguments are so frequent now that it is beginning to affect my college work and I am having to go to a friend's house to do my studying.

I really feel that the only sensible answer is for me to consider leaving home but that would be difficult as I don't get a grant. My friend's parents have said that I can go and lodge with them until I go to university in September but I don't know how to tell my parents or what the legal position would be with regard to me leaving home. By the way I am nearly eighteen years of age.

Andrew

Letter 4

Dear Maggie

I wouldn't like my mother to know that I had written this letter as I feel that she would be extremely hurt. I feel that she has given up a lot for me. My father died when I was a little girl and my mum has brought me up by herself but since I was about 10 years old she has suffered from multiple sclerosis.

First of all it wasn't too bad at all and she was able to go on doing most things but it's what they call a 'progressive' disease and over the last couple of years there is little doubt that things have got worse although she is still able to walk short distances.

The main problem is that although she never says that I can't go out with my friends I feel very guilty about leaving her alone. It really is beginning to affect my social life and I really don't know what to do about it because when I try to discuss it with my mum she just says that it is not a problem.

I finish college in a year's time and I am worried what will happen to her if I can't get a job close to home. Do you know if there's anyone or an organisation which might be able to help us?

Annette.

Letter 5

Dear Maggie and Tony

I am really worried about a close friend of mine because I think he may be taking drugs. He sometimes takes days off from college because he says that he just cannot be bothered but thats really because he just can't seem to be bothered to get up.

I have noticed that sometimes he is in a really 'high' mood but at others he seems really depressed and withdrawn not wanting to talk to anyone and his moods seem to change so quickly. Also on occasions I have noticed that his eyes seem to have a 'glazed' look about them.

The thing is I don't think his parents have any idea and I am not really certain although I have tried to talk to him about it but he just shrugs his shoulders and won't discuss the matter. But he doesn't deny that he might be taking drugs.

I feel that I ought to do something to help him or maybe at least let his family know. What do you think? So far I haven't done anything about it but I know that I should.

Mike.

Letter 6

Dear Tony

I am in my second year of a two year catering course at the college and I have one big, big problem which has hindered me all my life – SHYNESS. Just recently it has affected my life more than ever before because there's this really good looking guy in the first year of my course and I really fancy him and would love to go out with him. No, I am not cradle snatching because, although he is in the first year of my course, he is two years older than me.

My friends say that I should ask him out but I just can't pick up the courage. My friends just laugh at me and that just makes things ten times worse. Please help me. What do you think I should do? Would it be wrong of me to ask him out?

Siobhan

Letter 7

Dear Maggie

My boyfriend, who I have been going out with for the last three months wants me to sleep with him and I feel unsure about the whole thing.

In many ways I feel 'pressurised' because it is the 'thing' to do but I know that if my mum found out she would be furious because she is against sex before marriage.

I was thinking that perhaps I should go on the pill as I don't want to become pregnant but I'm worried that if I go to my family doctor for advice he might say something to my parents because he has been our doctor for a long time. I'm not even sure that the pill is the right form of contraception for me

I just feel totally confused about the whole thing. What do you think?

Pauline

Letter 8

Dear Tony and Maggie

I am coming to the end of a two year 'A' level course and would dearly love to study for a degree at university with a view to entering the teaching profession but my parents are totally opposed to the idea saying that there are already enough unemployed teachers as it is.

They want me to find a full time job in a bank when I leave college this summer as they think it will be a good, secure profession to enter but I want to persuade them otherwise. The other part of the problem is that they both work full time so I would not be entitled to a full grant and would need them to make some contribution to it.

Have you any ideas about how I could try to get them to change their minds?

Leroy

Letter 9

Dear Maggie

I'm sure you are going to say that you have heard this story before but I am writing to you in desperation. I'm pregnant – about two months. I have been to the doctor and had a pregnancy test which proved positive. I am seventeen years old and in the middle of a full time secretarial course.

I have told my boyfriend who is the father of the child and he seems just as confused about what we should do as I am. He's a full time college student as well.

My biggest worry is that if I tell my mother and father they will throw me out. This may sound silly but I just know they won't be sympathetic and helpful.

I really can't see any way of being able to keep the baby and I was wondering if it would be possible to have an abortion without my family knowing. I certainly don't want to get married and the prospect of bringing up a child alone just frightens me.

I keep turning the whole problem over and over in my mind and I just don't know who else to turn to for advice. Please what do you think I should do?

Angie

Letter 10

Dear Maggie and Tony

I am coming to the end of a YTS course which has been running at the college. I have been attending college for a 'block' period recently. I have been doing a course about different aspects of the retail trade.

There's no chance of a job with the firm which have been sponsoring me on the course and I don't have any formal qualifications. I'm really worried about being unemployed again because I know my parents will be mad. To make matters worse I have lied to them and said that I would be able to stay on working for the firm which are sponsoring me.

I really don't have any confidence and I feel I have no chance of a job. What can I do?

Hamid

Letter 11

Dear Tony

I am a day release student at the college and I work for a boat repair yard as a welder. I am twenty years of age and I would love to have a steady relationship with a girl but the problem is none of my relationships ever seem to last.

The longest I have ever been out with a girl was for six weeks and then she broke off the relationship. Most of my mates are either engaged or have steady girlfriends and I want to know where I am going wrong.

I am not particularly shy but I do find it quite difficult making conversation or approaching a girl to ask her out for the first time. Can you make any suggestions?

Jim

8 Penfield Film Club

AIM

To develop your skills in
* problem-solving in group situations

Introduction

This assignment is about trying to set up a film club in a college. From the various figures contained in the assignment you will find that there is a conflict of interest between what the students would like and what the college authorities are prepared to accept. Your main task is to try to arrive at a possible solution to the difficulty which will please as many people as possible.

A group of you have decided that it would be a good idea to start up a film club in the college. You have already done some preliminary work, such as writing to the Principal (Figure 1), sent away for a film catalogue (Figure 2), and carried out a survey among your fellow students to see how they feel about the idea (Figure 3).

Task 1

You decide to hold a meeting to discuss the present situation and to try to answer a number of points. Before the meeting it is important to have read Figures 1, 2 and 3. Here are the points you need to discuss:
(a) the rules and structure of the club;
(b) the time and day of film performances;
(c) the cost of membership (you cannot charge an admission fee – see Figure 2);
(d) the first term's film programme;
(e) exactly who is eligible for membership; and
(f) your response to the Principal's memo.

Task 2

The group has asked you to prepare a newspaper article for the college newsletter, outlining its ideas for the Film Club and seeking support from fellow students in making the venture a success.

The article should contain a headline, and be persuasive in tone.

Task 3

You have also been asked to design the membership card for the Film Club. The membership card must contain the following information:
(a) the name of the club, including its address and telephone number;
(b) the cost of the annual subscription;
(c) dates and times of performances, with the venue;
(d) a list of films to be shown, with their certificate rating (probably for one term); and
(e) rules of membership.

___**IMPORTANT**___
Read these information
pages:
A Committee meetings
E Writing articles

In addition there must be a place for the member's signature.

Your design should be laid out in the form of a draft for the printers, and the finished card should be pocket-sized.

Figure 1   Memorandum from the College Principal

MEMORANDUM

PENFIELD COLLEGE OF FURTHER EDUCATION

To: Film Club Organisers   **Ref:** KJF/ji

From: Mr. K. French, Principal   **Date:** 30 May 1986

Subject: Use of college premises and equipment

I welcome your initiative in trying to organise a film club for students of the college and I will endeavour to assist in any way that I can.

As regards the question of using college buildings and equipment, I have looked into the matter with the Administrative Officer and we can offer you the use of Lecture Theatre One, except on a Friday evening. This holds about one hundred and fifty people and contains the necessary equipment to show films. We can offer you this facility free of charge, as long as you vacate the building by 21.30 hours. If you wished to use the lecture theatre after this time you would have to pay for the caretaking staff to remain on the premises. This would cost you approximately seven pounds per hour, which would be charged as a number of complete hours (e.g. $2\frac{1}{2}$ hours would be charged as 3 hours).

We can also offer you the use of college equipment to show your films. However, the operation of this equipment would have to be handled by a college technician which will again cost you approximately seven pounds an hour if you wish to use the equipment after 21.30 hours.

As you will be using college facilities, I should draw your attention to Documents SC34 and SC35 (copies of which may be found in the General Office) which lay down the conditions (regarding health and safety, and so on) for the use of college premises.

I must also reserve the right to approve the rules of your club and to withdraw the use of college facilities if unsuitable material were to be shown. May I suggest that you seek my approval for any '18' rated film you may wish to show?

K French,

Figure 2   Extracts from a film catalogue

> **Film and Music Enterprises**
> **102 Bush Road**
> **London W1 8TX**
>
> **Tel: 01 866 3559**
>
> ---
>
> *Conditions of Licence*
>
> 1   The films may be exhibited during the period of the Licence at the venue(s) nominated in the Licence.
> 2   The films may *NOT* be exhibited to the general public nor may the licensed exhibitions be advertised to the general public.
> 3   Except with the express written consent of the film distributor *NO* admission charges may be made or other consideration asked from the audience.
> 4   The films must be exhibited in their entirety and the exhibitor shall ensure that appropriate equipment is used for exhibiting the films and that any such equipment is in good and efficient working order.
> 5   The exhibitor shall not exhibit the films otherwise than in strict accordance with the licence.
>
> *Key to Catalogue*
>
> Running time is indicated in minutes
> Hire time is the rate charged for 24-hour hire (excluding transportation cost)
> Black-and-white films indicated by *
> Foreign-language films indicated by **
>
> *Certification*
>
>   U = UNIVERSAL
>   PG = PARENTAL GUIDANCE
>   15 = ONLY FOR PERSONS OF FIFTEEN YEARS OF AGE AND
>   OVER
>   18 = ONLY FOR PERSONS OF EIGHTEEN YEARS OF AGE
>   AND OVER
>
> *Action and Adventure*
>
> | CATALOGUE NO. | TITLE | CERT. | RUNNING TIME | HIRE RATE |
> |---|---|---|---|---|
> | A 1001 | The African Queen | PG | 105 m | £30.00 |
> | A 1005 | Berlin Express | PG | 87 m | £25.00 |
> | A 1006 | Bullet for Rommel | PG | 100 m | £30.00 |
> | A 1012 | A Farewell to Arms* | U | 78 m | £30.00 |

CATALOGUE NO.	TITLE	CERT.	RUNNING TIME	HIRE RATE
A 1016	El Cid	U	180 m	£50.00
A 1019	The Fall of the Roman Empire	U	180 m	£50.00
A 1025	Fifty Five Days at Peking	U	140 m	£50.00
A 1037	King Kong*	PG	100 m	£35.00
A 1055	The Last Hunter	18	96 m	£45.00
A 1078	The Plough and the Stars	PG	72 m	£28.00
A 1079	Newsfront*	PG	110 m	£50.00
A 1083	Seven Samurai*	PG**	157 m	£50.00
A 1086	Slavers	18	100 m	£45.00

Charles Chaplin Films

C C01	The Kid*	U	53 m	£45.00
C C03	The Idle Class*	U	41 m	£45.00
C C05	The Gold Rush*	U	72 m	£65.00
C C09	Modern Times*	U	125 m	£65.00
C C10	The Great Dictator	U	125 m	£65.00
C C14	Monsieur Verdoux*	U	123 m	£65.00
C C15	Limelight*	U	135 m	£65.00

Charlie Chaplin in 'A King in New York' (1957)

CATALOGUE NO.	TITLE	CERT.	RUNNING TIME	HIRE RATE
Comedy				
C 1031	Don's Party	18	90 m	£40.00
C 1039	Eskimo Nell	18	90 m	£40.00
C 1047	Gas	15	79 m	£45.00
C 1048	The Groove Tube	18	73 m	£36.00
C 1051	How to Beat the High Cost of Living	15	97 m	£45.00
C 1054	Kentucky Fried Movie	18	84 m	£40.00
C 1075	Our Girl Friday*	U	75 m	£25.00
C 1088	Side by Side	PG	85 m	£30.00
C 1090	Ski Fever	PG	97 m	£25.00
C 1104	That Sinking Feeling	PG	112 m	£40.00
C 1107	Too Many Chefs	PG	90 m	£40.00
Drama				
D 1019	Dance Little Lady*	PG	88 m	£22.00
D 1020	Citizen Kane*	PG	119 m	£34.00
D 1022	Deep End	18	90 m	£32.00
D 1024	Despair	15	119 m	£50.00
D 1025	Diary of a Chambermaid*	PG	86 m	£30.00
D 1034	Golden Girl	PG	105 m	£40.00
D 1042	Heatwave	PG	93 m	£50.00
D 1056	Leopard in the Snow	PG	94 m	£35.00
D 1067	The Marriage of Maria Braun	15	120 m	£60.00
D 1069	My Brilliant Career	PG	98 m	£55.00
D 1070	My Girl Tina	PG	95 m	£22.00
D 1076	The Pawnbroker	18	113 m	£40.00
D 1078	Picnic at Hanging Rock	PG	115 m	£42.00
D 1080	Priest of Love	15	125 m	£48.00
D 1097	Roseland	PG	103 m	£40.00
D 1099	Savages	18	105 m	£40.00
Musicals				
M 1006	Birth of the Beatles	PG	108 m	£50.00
M 1007	Breaking Glass	15	104 m	£60.00
M 1017	Go, Johnny, Go	U	75 m	£38.00
M 1022	Elvis – the Movie	U	122 m	£55.00
M 1056	The Music Machine	U	90 m	£38.00
M 1066	Sympathy for the Devil	18	104 m	£40.00

CATALOGUE NO.	TITLE	CERT.	RUNNING TIME	HIRE RATE
M 1075	Oklahoma	U	121 m	£55.00
M 1089	The Road to Bali	U	90 m	£38.00
M 1097	Swing Time	U	85 m	£30.00
M 1109	Top Hat	U	108 m	£25.00

Mystery, Gangsters and Crime

CATALOGUE NO.	TITLE	CERT.	RUNNING TIME	HIRE RATE
G 1006	Al Capone*	PG	105 m	£40.00
G 1009	Assault on Precinct Thirteen	18	91 m	£46.00
G 1013	The Big Steal	PG	74 m	£24.00
G 1014	Atlantic City	15	105 m	£55.00
G 1017	Blood on the Sun*	PG	94 m	£24.00
G 1024	The Choirboys	18	122 m	£45.00
G 1029	Cry in the Night*	18	75 m	£35.00
G 1039	Daybreak*	PG**	93 m	£30.00
G 1042	Dillinger*	PG	70 m	£28.00
G 1050	Diva	15**	110 m	£55.00
G 1087	Mean Streets	18	110 m	£40.00
G 1093	The Next Man	PG	108 m	£47.00
G 1099	The Onion Field	18	126 m	£45.00
G 1118	The Silent Partner	18	105 m	£40.00
G 1132	Suspicion*	PG	100 m	£28.00

Science Fiction and Horror

CATALOGUE NO.	TITLE	CERT.	RUNNING TIME	HIRE RATE
H 1003	Attack of the Crab Monsters	PG	70 m	£35.00
H 1004	Attack of the Fifty-Foot Woman*	PG	65 m	£35.00
H 1014	Blood Beach	15	98 m	£39.00
H 1015	Billy the Kid versus Dracula	PG	84 m	£35.00
H 1018	The Broad	18	91 m	£50.00
H 1020	The Body Stealers	PG	91 m	£26.00
H 1021	The Body Snatcher*	PG	73 m	£22.00
H 1033	Count Dracula	18	98 m	£28.00
H 1037	Curse of the Cat People	PG	70 m	£22.00
H 1046	Doomwatch	PG	92 m	£27.00
H 1064	Halloween	18	91 m	£46.00
H 1065	Horror of Death	15	99 m	£38.00
H 1072	Invaders from Mars	PG	78 m	£38.00
H 1079	I Walked with a Zombie	PG	68 m	£32.00

CATALOGUE NO.	TITLE	CERT.	RUNNING TIME	HIRE RATE
H 1085	Jesse James meets Frankenstein's Daughter	PG	82 m	£35.00
H 1091	Kingdom of the Spiders	15	89 m	£35.00
H 1116	Scanners	18	103 m	£50.00
H 1123	The Thing from Another World	PG	87 m	£26.00

Westerns

W 1022	Blood River	18	97 m	£28.00
W 1045	Distant Drums	U	95 m	£28.00
W 1068	Fort Apache*	PG	127 m	£28.00
W 1080	My Name is Nobody	PG	115 m	£38.00
W 1100	Run of the Arrow	U	86 m	£30.00
W 1123	She Wore a Yellow Ribbon*	PG	100 m	£32.00

Literature in Film

L 1013	The Lost Moment*	PG	89 m	£30.00
L 1023	Ulysses*	18	132 m	£38.00
L 1044	The Birthday Party	18	124 m	£35.00
L 1047	Julius Caesar	U	117 m	£30.00
L 1051	Long Day's Journey into Night*	18	136 m	£40.00
L 1059	Macbeth*	PG	107 m	£35.00
L 1063	The Tempest	15	95 m	£55.00
L 1064	Under Milk Wood	15	91 m	£40.00
L 1065	Uncle Vanya*	PG	117 m	£38.00

Figure 3   Survey results

Results of survey carried out in the college between the 7th and 11th November concerning the setting up of a film club

Figure 3a   *Numbers involved in the survey (the figure represents approximately 5 per cent of total students attending college)*

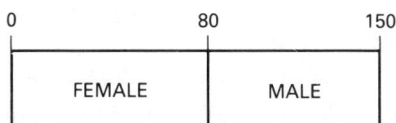

```
0              80        150
┌──────────────┬──────────┐
│   FEMALE     │   MALE   │
└──────────────┴──────────┘
```

Figure 3b   *Attitudes to the setting up of a film club*

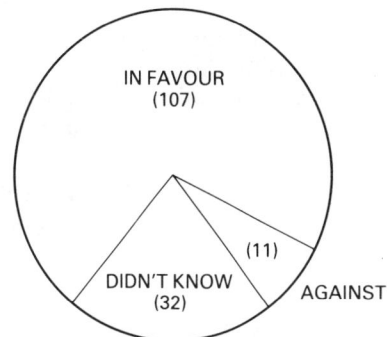

IN FAVOUR
(107)

(11)

DIDN'T KNOW
(32)

AGAINST

Figure 3c   *Expected attendance at such a club if set up*

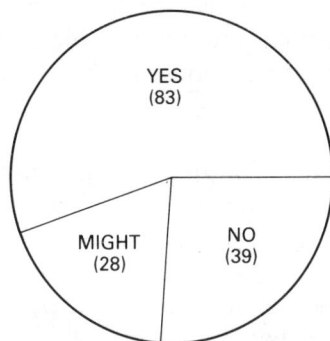

YES
(83)

MIGHT
(28)

NO
(39)

Figure 3d   *Nights of the week felt to be best for showing films*

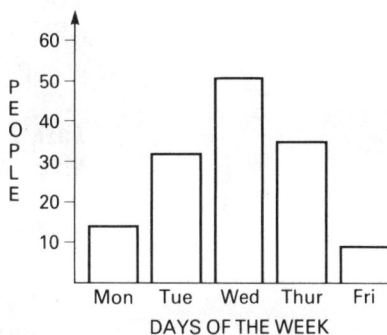

P
E
O
P
L
E

60
50
40
30
20
10

Mon   Tue   Wed   Thur   Fri
DAYS OF THE WEEK

Figure 3e   *Times felt to be best to start showing a film*

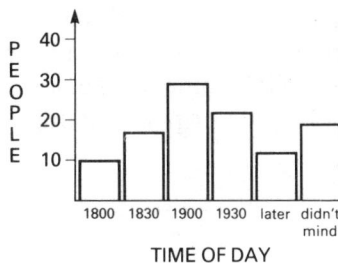

P
E
O
P
L
E

40
30
20
10

1800 1830 1900 1930 later didn't
                                mind
TIME OF DAY

Figure 3f   *Types of film preferred*

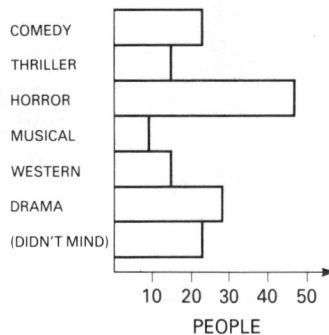

COMEDY
THRILLER
HORROR
MUSICAL
WESTERN
DRAMA
(DIDN'T MIND)

10   20   30   40   50
PEOPLE

Sponsored fun

9

To develop your skills in
● organisation and
  administration

Introduction

A few of you have decided that it might be a worthwhile idea to raise money for charity. Now you have to decide which is the best and most profitable way of raising money, and to which charity or charities the money should be donated.

Before you begin any of the tasks you should read Figures 1 and 2. If you want further information on any national or local charities, your college or local library will be able to help you.

Task 1

You have decided that the money could be raised by people sponsoring some kind of activity. Therefore your first task is:
(a) to suggest four or five activities which could be sponsored; and
(b) to suggest a few charities that could benefit from some of the money raised.

You should list the reasons for your choice of particular sponsored activities, so that you will be able to persuade other members of the group to accept your ideas at the meeting.

Task 2

Meet together as a group to put forward your ideas for sponsored activities and the charities that are to benefit from the money raised. Your group has to decide on the following:
(a) one sponsored activity for the group;
(b) the names of no more than three charities that will receive the money raised;
(c) how you will organise the sponsored activity, when it will take place, and who will participate; and
(d) how much you want each participant to collect.

Task 3

The group has asked you to design a leaflet, to be handed to students and members of the general public, telling them about the sponsored event and giving the name of a person whom they can contact if they are interested in helping or participating.

IMPORTANT

Read these information pages:
A Committee meetings
F Note making
H Leaflets

Figure 1 Some suggestions for sponsored events

The following list is a selection of possible sponsored activities – they are only suggestions, and you should use your own ideas if you prefer.

Sporting events that could be sponsored

Running
Walking
Dancing
Football
Jogging
Netball
Swimming
Hockey
Darts match
Basketball

Work-related events that could be sponsored

Typing
Cooking
Dismantling and reassembling a car
Hairdressing
Using a computer

Leisure-related events that could be sponsored

Playing cards
Car washing
Gardening
Sewing
Baby-sitting
Knitting
Window cleaning
Setting up a mile of pennies
Playing a musical instrument
Picking up litter

Figure 2   Some national charities that you might wish to consider sponsoring

1   Guide Dogs for the Blind Association
9–11 Park Street
Windsor
Berkshire

2   The Royal National Institute for the Blind (RNIB)
224 Great Portland Street
London W1N 6AA

3   The Royal National Institute for the Deaf (RNID)
105 Gower Street
London WC1F 6AH

4   The National Deaf Children's Society
45 Hereford Road
London W2 5AH

5   Association for Spina Bifida and Hydrocephalus
Tavistock House North
Tavistock Square
London WC1H 9HJ

6   The Multiple Sclerosis Society of Great Britain and Northern
Ireland
286 Munster Road
London SW6 6AP

7   The Spastics Society
12 Park Crescent
London W1N 4EQ

8   MIND (National Association for Mental Health)
22 Harley Street
London W1N 2FD

9   MENCAP (National Society for Mentally Handicapped Children)
123 Golden Lane
London EC1Y 0RT

10   The Samaritans
17 Uxbridge Road
Slough SL1 1SN

11   British Heart Foundation Appeal
102 Gloucester Road
London W1H 4DH

12   Cancer Research Campaign
2 Carlton House Terrace
London SW1Y 5AR

13 The Leprosy Mission
50 Portland Place
London W1N 3DG

14 Leukaemia Research Fund
43 Great Ormond Street
London WC1N 3JJ

15 Doctor Barnardo's
Tanners Lane
Barkingside
Ilford
Essex IG6 1PQ

16 National Children's Homes (NCH)
85 Highbury Park
London N5 1UD

17 National Society for the Prevention of Cruelty to Children (NSPCC)
1 Riding House Street
London W1Q 8AA

18 Save the Children Fund (SCF)
17 Grove Lane
London SE5 8RD

19 The National Trust (NT)
Queen Anne's Gate
London SW1H 9AS

20 Health Education Council
78 New Oxford Street
London WC1A 1AH

21 Royal Life-Saving Society
Mountbatten House
Dudley
Warwickshire B80 7NN

22 Royal Society for the Prevention of Cruelty to Animals (RSPCA)
The Causeway
Horsham
Sussex RH12 1HG

23 Royal National Lifeboat Institution (RNLI)
West Quay Road
Poole
Dorset BH15 1HZ

These names and addresses were extracted from *The Charities Digest* (19th edition) 1984.

10 The law decides

AIM

To develop your skills in
- making decisions
- recognising the effects of decisions on other people

Introduction

For the purpose of this assignment, you have to put yourself in the position of a magistrate in a court who has various offenders before him or her. It is your role to decide on the appropriate sentence for each individual case.

In a Magistrates' Court, the Bench, which normally consists of three people (two ordinary members and a Chairperson), is made up of men and women from the community. They are nominated for service as a magistrate by various local organisations, and go through a short period of training before they can actually 'sit' on the bench. They are not paid for doing this job but receive 'out of pocket' expenses. For example, if they are likely to lose income from their normal job by having to attend court for a day, then they will be paid the equivalent of a normal day's salary.

When the court is in session, the magistrates are advised on points of law by a Clerk of the Court who helps to ensure that they do not make any mistakes when exercising their sentencing powers. The Clerk of the Court is a full-time court official.

£200 fine <u>and</u> a criminal record.

If you evade your fare on the Buses or Tubes you could be fined up to £200 or more – and get a criminal record. Something that could affect the rest of your life.

Get the right ticket, not a criminal record.

Figure 1 contains extracts of information about the offences that the people coming before the court have committed. Each case study contains some background information about each offender, including his or her occupation, education and social background, and details about any previous offences which he or she may have committed. You should take all these factors into account when deciding what is the most appropriate sentence.

Figure 2 contains a list of possible sentences that the bench could give to each offender.

Task 1

Your first task is to imagine that you are one of the magistrates sitting in the court. You have to decide which is the most appropriate sentence for each of the five offenders coming before you. In note form, give your reasons for choosing that particular sentence, and your reasons for rejecting the other possible sentences.

Task 2

Using the notes which you prepared in Task 1 you should now meet as a group (probably no more than six in a group) and agree on one sentence for each of the five offenders. It may take quite a bit of discussion before you can reach a *majority* decision. Before attempting this task, you will probably find it helpful to appoint one member of the group as Chairperson of the Bench.

____**IMPORTANT**____

Read these information pages:
A Committee meetings
F Note making

Figure 1   Extracts from court reports

```
Case 1: MR S.

NAME:  Mr S.
AGE:  20 years of age.
MARITAL STATUS:  Single.
OCCUPATION:  Mr S is currently employed as a carpenter
   with a firm of local builders. He has recently
   finished his apprenticeship with them.
THE CHARGES:  Driving with excess alcohol.
              Unaccompanied learner driver.
              No 'L' plates.
              No insurance.
              Bald tyres.
              Faulty headlamps.
THE OFFENCE:  The police stated that they saw Mr S
   driving in an erratic manner along a main road at
   about 2300 hours. They stopped him and asked him to
   get out of his car. He was given a breath test and the
```

intoximeter showed that he had 100 milligrams of
alcohol to 100 millilitres of blood, which is above
the legal amount. He was further charged with driving
a car unaccompanied whilst holding only a provisional
licence, with not displaying 'L' plates, and with
driving a vehicle whilst being uninsured. The Datsun
Cherry that he was driving at the time of the offence
was found to have two defective front tyres and
headlights that did not work properly.

EDUCATION: Mr S attended a large, local comprehensive
school where he gained four CSEs. He left at sixteen
years of age. He did not particularly enjoy school and
was quite glad when it was time to leave.

FAMILY BACKGROUND: Mr S comes from a family of six
children of which he is the eldest. His father left
his mother when Mr S was twelve years old. The family
has had no contact with the father since.

Mr S still lives at home with his family and makes a
large financial contribution to help his mother bring
up the rest of the family all of whom are still at
school.

MR S's COMMENTS: On the night of the offence Mr S said
that he had been out with his girlfriend to a local
pub and that she had decided to break off their
relationship. He was upset and annoyed about this and
after taking her home he had gone to have another
couple of drinks. It was after this that he had been
stopped by the police.

He said that he is also unhappy at home and finding
it a struggle having to give his mother so much of his
money towards running the home. He feels that he has
much less money than his friends.

Case 2: Mr E.

NAME: Mr E.
AGE: 47 years of age.
MARITAL STATUS: Married.
OCCUPATION: Unemployed.
THE CHARGES: Causing actual bodily harm.
             Drunk and disorderly.
THE OFFENCE: The police were called to the home of
Mr E's wife in the early hours of the morning. Mr

E was drunk and had broken the glass in the front door of the house in order to gain access. His wife, now living with another man, was absolutely terrified and Mr E became very aggressive when his wife refused to let him see their ten-year-old daughter, and punched his wife on the nose. The police were called, arrested him, and took him to the police station where he was charged.

EDUCATION: Mr E had secondary-modern-school education, leaving school at fifteen years of age without gaining any formal qualifications.

FAMILY BACKGROUND: Mr E has been married to his wife for fifteen years and they have one ten-year-old daughter of that marriage.

His wife has recently obtained a court injunction to prevent him entering the marital home because on at least three occasions, late at night, he has made drunken scenes outside the family home and the police have had to be called.

Mr E is now living in a bed-sitter and is claiming unemployment benefit.

He used to work as a storekeeper but has not been in any form of regular employment for the last eighteen months.

His wife feels that most of their problems have been caused by his persistent, heavy drinking. She has now formed a stable relationship with another man and says that she will not have her husband back under any circumstances.

PREVIOUS OFFENCES: During the past three years Mr E has been before the court twice on charges of being drunk and disorderly.

He also has one conviction for theft of £250.00.

MR E's COMMENTS: Mr E said that he has found it hard to come to terms with his recent separation and misses seeing his little girl. This situation has now been aggravated by the court injunction.

He also recognised the fact that he has quite a severe drink problem and any spare cash he has goes on buying more drink. He does not think that he needs any professional help with his drink problem.

Case 3: MRS P.

NAME: Mrs P.

AGE: 68 years of age.

MARITAL STATUS: Widow.

OCCUPATION: Old-age pensioner.

THE CHARGE: Theft.

THE OFFENCE: The store detective at a local department store called the police to the Store Manager's office where Mrs P was waiting. The store detective said that she had watched Mrs P shopping in the store and that she had taken two jumpers from the counter and, when no one was looking, had placed them in her own shopping bag without paying for them. The value of the goods was £19.98. She allowed Mrs P to leave the store and outside asked her to open her bag and produce a receipt for the goods. Mrs P was unable to do so. The store detective took her to the Manager's office and called the police. Mrs P was subsequently charged, by the police, with theft.

FAMILY BACKGROUND: Mrs P has been a widow for about three years. She has a married son and a daughter who do not live locally.

She lives in a large, detached house and has no financial worries. She is a very outgoing, sociable lady who belongs to several local clubs as well as doing voluntary work at the hospital, and is a member of the WRVS (Women's Royal Voluntary Service).

MRS P's COMMENTS: She was very concerned about this offence and said that she could not remember anything about it and was astonished when the store detective found the jumpers in her shopping bag. She said she can offer no logical explanation.

Her main worry was that this offence would be reported in the local newspaper and would be a dreadful disgrace for herself and her family.

Case 4: MR T.

NAME: Mr T.

AGE: 18 years of age.

MARITAL STATUS: Single.

OCCUPATION: Unemployed since leaving school.

THE CHARGE: Burglary.

THE OFFENCE: It is alleged by the police that Mr T
   entered a house while both the occupants were at work,
   and stole cash and jewellery to the value of £145.47.
   He gained access to the house by climbing through an
   open back window, and was spotted by a sharp-eyed
   neighbour who reported the suspected break-in to the
   police. As a result of her action, Mr T was
   apprehended by the police two days later and was
   charged with burglary.

EDUCATION: Mr T attended a comprehensive school where
   he was described by his teachers as a potentially
   bright young person, but his main problem seemed to be
   lack of interest. By the time he was fourteen there
   were considerable attendance problems, and the
   Education Welfare Service was involved. He was
   eventually sent to a special centre for children
   suffering from school 'phobia'. He left school with no
   formal educational qualifications.

FAMILY BACKGROUND: Mr T comes from a stable family home,
   but his relationship with his parents was never very
   good and he left home when he was seventeen years old
   to live in his own bed-sitter.

   He has one sister, who is fourteen years old, but he
   hardly has any contact with his family.

PREVIOUS OFFENCES: Over the past two years Mr T has
   received two other convictions for petty theft. He has
   already spent some time in a detention centre.

MR T's COMMENTS: He said that he did not really care
   about this further offence and that he needed to have
   some 'ready' cash as he was behind with the rent.

   He felt that there are no incentives for him to
   obtain regular employment, and he is happy to spend
   the day hanging around with his friends who find
   themselves in a similar position.

Case 5: MRS M.

NAME: Mrs M.

AGE: 29 years of age.

MARITAL STATUS: Separated.

OCCUPATION: Part-time barmaid.

THE CHARGE: Making false representations.

THE OFFENCE: Mrs M is accused of making false representations in order to obtain supplementary benefit. The Department of Health and Social Security estimate that they have overpaid her by approximately £300. She has apparently been working as a barmaid at a local public house in the evenings and has not been declaring her earnings to the Department.

EDUCATION: Mrs M attended a local grammar school, which she left at sixteen years of age with three 'O' levels.

FAMILY BACKGROUND: Mrs M has three children, aged six years, four years and eighteen months. Her ex-husband is the father of her eldest child and the other two children are by different boyfriends.

She lives on supplementary benefit in a three-bedroom council house, but since the offence against the DHSS, she has lost her part-time job. She is separated from her former husband who is unable to make any financial contribution towards keeping the children as he is unemployed and has a drug problem.

PREVIOUS OFFENCES: Over the last three years Mrs M has been convicted of theft and of raiding her electricity meter. For the first offence she received a probation order for a year and for the second offence she received a three-month suspended prison sentence. She is currently not in breach of either sentence.

MRS M's COMMENTS: She said that she finds it a continual struggle to make ends meet and hates to see her children suffer.

She knows that she should have reported the extra earnings to the DHSS but says that all the money she obtained was spent on clothes, food and extras for the children. She says that she is sorry for the trouble caused but admits that she does not seem to have learned from previous sentences.

Figure 2   Extracts from notes supplied to the Magistrates by the Clerk of the Court

What follows is information for magistrates' guidance concerning maximum sentencing powers for each offence and any other information considered necessary to help magistrates in their decision.

Case 1: MR S.
OFFENCE: Driving with excess alcohol.
PENALTY: Minimum 12 months automatic disqualification, plus a fine up to a maximum of £2000.00 and/or up to a maximum of six months' imprisonment. Licence endorsed.
OFFENCE: Unaccompanied learner driver.
PENALTY: Maximum fine £400.00. Disqualification from driving discretionary. Licence endorsed. Two penalty points*.
OFFENCE: No 'L' plates.
PENALTY: Maximum fine £400.00. Disqualification discretionary. Licence endorsed. Two penalty points*.
OFFENCE: No insurance.
PENALTY: Maximum fine £1000.00. Disqualification discretionary. Licence endorsed. Four to eight penalty points*.
OFFENCE: Defective tyres.
PENALTY: Maximum fine £1000.00. Disqualification discretionary. Licence endorsed. Three penalty points*.
OFFENCE: Defective headlamps.
PENALTY: Maximum fine £400.00.

* If for any charge the driver is disqualified then penalty points are ignored.

Case 2: MR E.
OFFENCE: Causing actual bodily harm*.
PENALTY: Maximum fine £2000.00 and/or up to six months' imprisonment**.
OFFENCE: Drunk and disorderly.
PENALTY: Maximum fine £200.00.
OFFENCE: Breach of the peace.
PENALTY: Bound over. (This means that the offender is committed to keeping the peace for a period of time specified by the court.)

* Such an offence can be tried in a Crown Court by judge and jury if the defendant so wishes.
** If any sentence carries the possibility of

imprisonment, the magistrate has various other options
that could be used rather than committing an offender to
such an institution. These are:
  (a) conditional discharge to the maximum of three
      years;
  (b) probation to the maximum of three years; and
  (c) community service (order up to a maximum of 240
      hours).

Case 3: MRS P.
OFFENCE: Theft*.
PENALTY: Maximum £2000.00 fine and/or up to six months'
  imprisonment. Magistrates can also award compensation
  up to a maximum of £2000.00.

* See both case notes on Mr E.

Case 4: MR T.
OFFENCE: Burglary*.
PENALTY: Maximum fine £2000.00 and/or up to six months'
  imprisonment. As with the case of Mrs P, compensation
  can be awarded. Magistrates should also be aware that
  burglary (which is theft from a dwelling house) is
  considered more serious than ordinary theft (which is
  theft from a non-dwelling house), and worse still if
  the owners are in residence at the time of burglary.

* See both case notes on Mr E.

Case 5: MRS M.
OFFENCE: Making false representations*.
PENALTY: Maximum fine £1000.00 and/or up to three
  months' imprisonment.

* See both case notes on Mr E.

Focus assignments

11 Lytchett Engineering plc

AIM

To develop your skills in
- writing effectively for a specific audience
- decision making

Introduction

An important and vital function in any large firm is that of the Personnel Department. Not only does the department deal with workers' problems and with industrial relations but it is also concerned with training personnel.

This assignment places you in the position of an Assistant Personnel Manager concerned principally with staff training, and involves you in a variety of communication tasks connected with such a post.

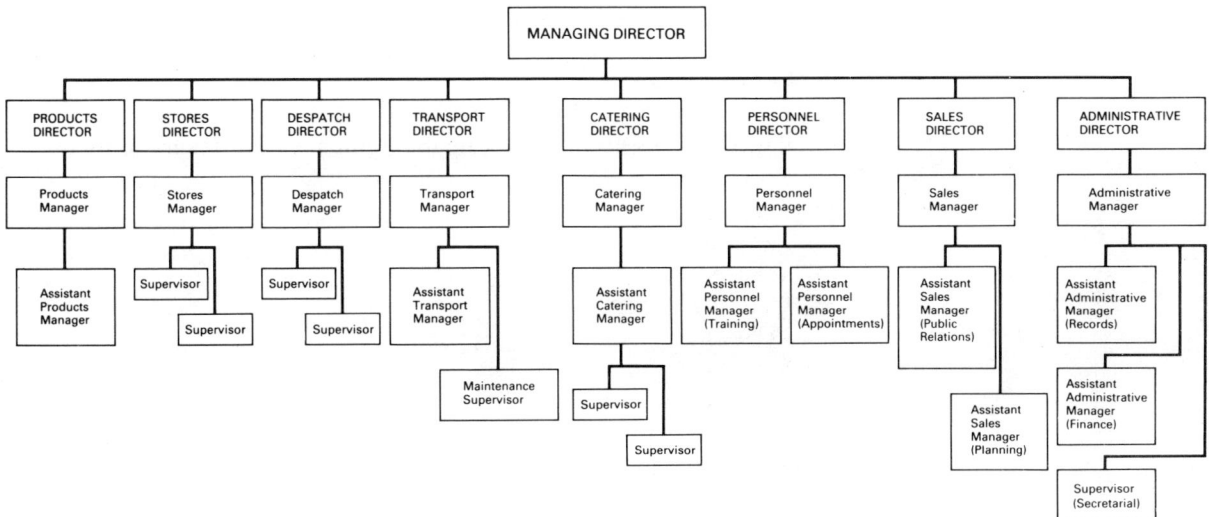

Task 1

Read Figures 1–4. Then write the newspaper article, for inclusion in the company magazine, which your boss has asked for (in Figure 2).

Task 2

Following the publication of your article your boss has asked you and other members of the Personnel Department concerned with staff training to meet. You are to discuss and design the structure and format of a one-week induction course which will introduce all new employees to Lytchett Engineering plc.

You will need to decide on a definite programme for the course, and what visits and lectures you are going to include each day. Each member of the committee will need to make notes outlining the induction programme, to assist them in completing Task 3.

COLLEGE LIBRARY
COLLEGE OF TECHNOLOGY
CARNARVON ROAD
SOUTHEND-ON-SEA, ESSEX

IMPORTANT

Read these information pages:

A Committee meetings
E Writing articles
H Leaflets

Figure 1 Extracts from past in-house magazine articles

Task 3

The Personnel Manager has accepted your committee's ideas and programme for the induction week, and she has now asked you to prepare a draft brochure for the printers. This brochure will be sent to all new employees joining the company. It should aim to tell new employees a little bit about the company, but its main aim should be to tell them about the week's induction programme.

. . . The firm was started in 1895 by Laurence Lytchett to make parts for agricultural machinery. Later, Lytchetts moved into the production of engine parts for the automobile industry, especially cam shafts. By 1934 the firm had become a public company and was employing about one hundred people. . . .

. . . In the 1980s the firm is moving into the technological age by combining engine-part production with high-precision engineering for the French aerospace industry. . . .

. . . The firm has a Board of Directors; each director controls one of the eight departments that make up the Company. The departments are:

(a) Production;
(b) Stores;
(c) Despatch;
(d) Transport;
(e) Catering;
(f) Personnel;
(g) Sales; and
(h) Administration.

The directors are responsible for the overall policy of the firm, but the actual day-to-day running of each department is in the hands of a manager, who is assisted by either assistant managers or supervisors. . . .

. . . The factory is of a fairly modern design, having been built in 1965, and covers a site of some five hectares. . . .

. . . The factory is located on a trading estate on the outskirts of the town. The buildings include not only the factory and administrative offices but also the social club and canteen. In the grounds there are two tennis courts, and a large field which is used for football in winter and cricket in summer. . . .

. . . The non-clerical workforce starts at 8.00 a.m., has one hour for lunch and finishes at 5.00 p.m. Most employees work a thirty-nine-hour week. . . .

. . . Clerical staff are on flexi-time, working a thirty-six-hour week. All employees are allowed two paid ten-minute tea breaks each day. . . .

. . . The firm has always been keen on employing young workers at the start of their careers. In fact the present Managing Director started out as an apprentice with the firm, on the shop floor, twenty years ago. . . .

. . . Lytchetts have also always been keen on training that not only caters for the specific needs of the firm, but that also provides the young worker with an opportunity to develop new skills. To further this aim the firm has always liaised closely with the local College of Further Education. . . .

. . . The firm is in the process of designing a one-week induction course for all new employees. It is hoped that such a course will not only provide information about the Company but will also provide employees with an overall working knowledge of the whole Company, rather than just a small section of it. . . .

. . . The management envisages that the induction programme will include some of the following ideas:

(a) the history and structure of the Company;
(b) some knowledge of each department's function, both in theory and in practice;
(c) an introduction to training opportunities within the Company, including a visit to the local Further Education College;
(d) an introduction to the Company's social facilities; and
(e) an introduction to the Company Pension Scheme.

Figure 2 Memorandum from the Personnel Manager

MEMO

LYTCHETT ENGINEERING PLC

To: Assistant Personnel Manager (Training)   **Date:** 25th May 1986

From: Mrs A. Etherington, Personnel Manager   **Ref:** AE/RS

Subject: Training for young employees

I have been asked by Head Office to supply a four-hundred-word article, for inclusion in the next edition of the in-house magazine, on the above topic.

As you are principally concerned with this area of training, would you please let me have a suitable draft article for this purpose, by 16th June? Thanks for your help.

Andrea Etherington

Figure 3 Statistical information about Lytchetts' employees

Figure 3a *Numbers working at Lytchett Engineering PLC*

Departments	Male	Female
Production	253	7
Stores	15	10
Despatch	15	15
Transport	9	1
Catering	0	6
Personnel	5	7
Sales	9	6
Administration	5	27
TOTAL	311	79

Figure 3b *Age distribution of workforce*

Age groups	Male	Female
16–20	35	10
21–30	62	32
31–40	75	6
41–50	78	16
51–60	36	15
61–65	25	–

Figure 3c *Distribution by department of the 16–20 age group*

Department	Male	Female
Production	27	2
Stores	2	0
Despatch	3	2
Transport	2	0
Catering	0	1
Personnel	0	0
Sales	1	0
Administration	0	5
TOTAL	35	10

Figure 4   Extract from a report on Lytchetts' present training programme for young employees

Department	No. of Trainees	Type of training being undertaken
Production	29	(a) 2 employees doing one year's full-time training at local FE college (b) 6 first-year engineering YTS students: half-time at work and half-time at local FE college (c) 9 second-year engineering apprentices on day-release (d) 12 third-year apprentices on day-release
Transport	2	(a) 1 first-year YTS trainee on day-release at FE college (b) 1 mechanic on a technician day-release course
Catering	1	(a) 1 first-year trainee on block-release scheme for chefs: six weeks at college, three weeks at work for first eighteen months of training
Stores/despatch	7	(a) 2 first-year employees full-time at FE college on stock-handling course (b) 2 second-year trainees on day-release courses at FE college (c) 3 third-year employees on day-release courses
Administration/sales	6	(a) 1 first-year YTS trainee: half-time at work and half-time at local FE college on a secretarial course (b) 2 second-year employees on day-release accounts' clerk courses (c) 3 third-year employees on day-release courses to train in the use of word processors

12 New site for Olds

AIM

To develop your written and graphic skills in
- presenting decisions
- selecting information

Introduction

Old UK plc are industrial drilling-machine manufacturers, based just outside Ipswich. Their main concern at the moment is where to site a new additional factory which will make computer-controlled drilling machines. The Board of Directors has decided to hold a special meeting to discuss this one topic and to arrive at a decision about where to locate the new factory. As a member of the Board, it is your task to evaluate the suitability of the proposed sites and with the help of your fellow directors to come to a decision about which site would best suit the company's needs.

The board has had a report compiled on each of the sites (see Figure 3). It is advisable to study *all* relevant figures before attempting *any* of the tasks.

Task 1

It is necessary before attending the Board Meeting to be familiar with the advantages and disadvantages of the possible locations for the new factory. Your first task therefore is to compile a set of notes outlining the possible benefits and limitations of each of the proposed sites.

To help you with this task a sample grid is provided. You can copy and use this to help you draw the necessary conclusions from the information provided in the figures.

Grid to determine advantages and disadvantages of site locations

	Site location		Site location	
	Advantages	Disadvantages	Advantages	Disadvantages
Workforce				
Transport/ markets				
Raw materials				
Costs				
Communications				

Task 2

You meet as a Board to decide on the location of your new factory.

Task 1 will have shown you that all sites have factors that commend them, but the Board has to decide which it feels are the important factors to be taken into account when reaching its decision about which is the best site. Figure 2 gives a brief explanation of the factors influencing the location of an industry in a particular area.

___**IMPORTANT**___

Read these information pages:
A Committee meetings
F Note making
I Circular letters

Task 3

Your final task, once the decision about the site has been made, is to prepare a circular letter to be distributed to your employees explaining your decision, the reasons behind the siting of the new factory, and how its location will affect them.

Figure 1 Newspaper article

Forty years 'Old' and still going strong

Old UK plc will be celebrating forty years of trading this year. The firm, one of the largest in the area, will not only be celebrating past successes, but will also be toasting the future.

Olds started forty years ago, just after the end of World War II, when three friends pooled their 'demob' money and started up a small workshop in Trinity Road, making drilling machines for the engineering industry. Helped by the expansion and changeover of industry from armament to commercial production, the company soon grew, and by 1955 it had moved from Trinity Road to the London Road Industrial Estate and was employing five hundred local people. During the 'you've never had it so good' fifties the company continued its successful rise – so much so that, by 1960, it had expanded its factory at London Road and was employing nearly 2000 workers.

Swinging sixties

While the Beatles were taking the entertainment world by storm and British industry was beginning to stagnate, Olds was entering pastures new. Forward planning by the directors, and a willingness on the part of the workforce to accept new ideas, led the company away from an over-dependence on the home market for sales and, long before Britain, Olds was in Europe. So successful was this sales drive to capture the European engineering industry that by 1970, 40 per cent of Olds total production was destined for the countries of Europe. Olds is today one of the foremost names amongst middle-sized firms in the Common Market.

Hi-tech and Olds

The 1970s and 1980s have, yet again, seen Olds in the forefront of developments. Olds has always been a company that has placed considerable store by research and development, and this has certainly paid dividends over the last decade.

Olds was one of the first engineering manufacturers to produce computer-controlled machines (CCMs). They have benefited from this lead. Alongside their factory in London Road they now have a unit employing some three hundred people producing the hi-tech elements for their CCMs. A company spokesman told me, 'this is the future for Old plc'. The disturbing fact is that most of their CCMs are for export. The same spokesman estimated that about 75 per cent of all their CCM production was destined for Europe.

The future

The future for Olds seems rosy. Not only has it conquered Europe, it is now planning to expand into America and the Far East. A company spokesman told me that the company hopes that by 1995, 50 per cent of total production will be for these markets. When asked if this meant expansion of the operation in the local area he stated: 'Old UK have no intention of leaving the area. However, our present site is becoming cramped and there are difficulties in expanding it.'

So while Old UK plc celebrates forty years, the local community waits to see what Olds and the future holds in store for them.

Figure 2   Some factors influencing the location of industry

1   Communication

Once a company expands to more than one site, the difficulty of communicating information, instructions and other data becomes more of a problem. Distance, even in our technological age, still means the increasing use of paper and other methods of recording information. There is also the problem of personnel. Unless a firm is going to duplicate every single post or function, then a degree of staff movement from one site to another is essential. Any new location has to take these factors into consideration.

2   Costs

Costs are always important to industry because they determine the price of the product. Costs of a new site not only include such obvious items as land, buildings and machinery, but also such costs as local labour which not only involve wages but may also include such items as travel and housing costs. This applies particularly if the firm wishes to take specialised labour with it to a new location. Development areas normally have financial incentives to attract new industry to the area. These incentives include such items as attractive planning regulations, low rates, help with housing for 'key' workers, and other financial benefits.

3   Raw materials

These are also an important element in a firm's costings. They include not only the cost of the materials themselves but also the costs of transporting these to the site and of handling them. Also included in this section is the cost of the stocks of raw materials that the firm has to keep in reserve, and, at the other end of the production process, the costs involved in stocking finished items and large quantities of spare parts.

4   Transport and markets

Just as it costs money to transport raw materials to the factory, so it costs money to transport finished products to the customer. To assess the appropriateness of a particular site, two elements need to be considered:
(a) where the customers are located; and
(b) the nature of the product.
Both factors will determine the type of transport it is cheapest to use. For example, small products can be effectively transported over short distances by road, whereas larger items might necessitate the use of rail or shipping facilities.

5   Workforce

This is perhaps one of the most important costs an industrialist has to deal with. The workforce is one of the key elements to any firm's success. A good workforce is secured not only with fair financial reward but with an effective personnel-management team. The location of a firm also affects the workforce – for example, some parts of the country have a stronger trades-union tradition than other parts. Your firm may need skilled labour; certain skills tend to be more abundant in some parts of the country than others. If skilled labour is in short supply, then its price is likely to be high.

Figure 3   Extracts from site location reports

Figure 3a   *Report on Bristol site*

... The site is situated just outside Bristol at the industrial complex of Avonmouth....

... The area has long been involved with the engineering industry and this means that the necessary skilled labour would be **available**. However, there would be competition for such labour from other engineering firms in the area. **This means that labour might prove expensive....**

... The area is well suited for the recruitment of highly qualified personnel: it contains not only a university but also a polytechnic, specialising in producing highly qualified engineers....

... The fact that Avonmouth is a port would mean that the importation of the necessary raw materials would present no problems. However the fact that most of our steel at the moment comes from Sweden could mean that transportation costs would rise. This increase could be offset by switching to British steel, which at the moment is slightly more expensive, but which would be competitive at the Bristol site if transported by rail from the Midlands....

... The other raw material, namely computer parts, should not be affected by the move to this site as our suppliers are located in the Southampton area; the transportation costs from there to Bristol would be no more than from Southampton to Ipswich....

... The fact that the new site is being developed to produce drilling machines for export, especially for America and the Far East, means that any site should take account of facilities for exporting our finished product to those areas. The products are bulky and the only pratical method of shipment is by sea. Avonmouth, being an international port, is therefore an ideal location, and its location on the west coast of the British Isles makes it one of the cheapest of the four sites as regards transportation costs to the Far East and America....

... The area is served not only by an international port but also by good road and rail links. This means that communication between Ipswich and Avonmouth should present no major problems. This is especially true in the area of personnel communication between the two sites. The motorway and the inter-city rail link means a journey between sites to solve urgent problems of about three hours.... Key personnel would also probably be willing to move to an area like Bristol....

... A major disadvantage of the proposed location is the actual cost of the site.... It has been suggested that it would be cheaper to lease a factory already built than to buy the land and build. Even so, compared to the other three sites, this area is expensive.... A further limitation of the site is that there is very little room for future expansion within the same location....

... Given the high cost of leasing a factory and the possible high cost of labour, the unit cost of our product might prove to high, especially if we wished to break into new markets, where a major factor in getting our product off the ground will be its price....

Figure 3b   *Report on Glasgow site*

... The area suffers high unemployment problems, especially in engineering-related skills, therefore the recruitment of a labour force would present little problem. However, like the Newcastle area, trade unionism is strong in the region and the company would need to deal fully and carefully with conditions of employment and with potential labour-relations difficulties. The area is also developing its own computer industries, therefore this form of labour would be available, but because of competition would be likely to be expensive....

... This site is the cheapest of the four. Like the Newcastle Council, the Scottish Economic Development Council (SEDC) is keen to attract our type of firm to the area, which means that financial concessions are available. However, even with these concessions there is still only about £200 000 between the cheapest site, Glasgow, and the most expensive site, Ipswich....

... Transport should present no great problem. The port is well placed for exporting to America, though the same cannot be said for exports to the Far East....

... Raw materials should not present any difficulty; in fact they might prove to be significantly cheaper. Swedish steel might well be slightly cheaper if shipped to Glasgow, and computer parts could prove cheaper still. This is because the area is trying to develop its own computer-production plants, which would mean that we could buy the parts locally, resulting in a major saving in transport costs. However, this is still only a possibility: if the industry did not develop then costs would rise, as we would have to transport the parts all the way from Southampton....

... Communications could be the other main problem. Although the area has access to motorways, airports and rail networks, it is still a considerable distance from our main centre of operation in Ipswich. This would involve staff in much more travelling time, and could result in delays in getting problems sorted out, especially if top management were needed in person. It might also be a problem to get 'key' personnel to move such a distance, and financial compensations for staff could be considerable, which would add to the unit costs of production....

Figure 3c *Report on Ipswich site*

... Obviously this site would present us with the fewest
communications problems, although the new factory would not be
situated on the same site as our present factory, but three miles
further south on a new industrial estate. It would mean that the
expertise and good relations we have built up in the town could be
put to good use. It would be possible to have only one branch of
top management running both sites. It would mean that the function
of key people would be much more available as they could easily
move between sites with much less disruption to their personal and
working lives....

... The use of this location would also mean no change as far as
raw-material costs are concerned. Steel coming to the port of
Ipswich would cost just as much for the new factory as the old.
The same applies to computer parts....

... A major problem could arise from shortage of labour: although
unemployment in the Ipswich area is high, most of it tends to be in
the field of semi-skilled or unskilled labour. This could mean
significantly higher labour costs, either because we would have to
import labour from further afield or because we would have to spend
money on expensive training programmes....

... Being near London it would be possible for us to attract the
high-calibre computer engineers we will be looking for....

... Like Newcastle upon Tyne, Ipswich is on the east coast of
England, which means that transportation costs for finished
products would vary depending on the market we aimed to develop
first. However, unlike Newcastle, it will be much cheaper to send
goods to the Far East....

... The cost of this location would be the highest of the four.
This is because we have not only to build the factory from scratch
but to buy the land on which it would stand. However, this may not
be as bad as it at first seems. The site is much larger than is
required for present plans, which gives us two advantages – room
for expansion, and room to store finished goods. Thus although the
site might be the most expensive, it is also the site with the most
possibilities for the future....

Figure 3d *Report on Newcastle upon Tyne site*

... One of the important factors in considering this location is
the cost of building a factory in the **area.** Because the area
suffers from the blight of high unemployment, the local authority
is keen to attract new industry to the area, so special concessions
are available as far as planning and costs are concerned. This
means that the development of a factory site would be relatively
cheap; in fact only the location at Glasgow proves cheaper....
... The recruitment of labour would also prove no problem. Not only
is the area suffering from a high degree of unemployment, but much
of this is among engineering workers, although it is thought that
some degree of retraining would be necessary and negotiation with
local trade unions would be essential as this is traditionally a
militant union area, but again these points need not prove to be
serious obstacles....
... Although this site is about three hundred miles, by road, from
our main centre of operations at Ipswich, it has good
communications in terms of rail, road and airport facilities.
However, there might be difficulties in getting quick decisions on
major problems and it might prove necessary to move a greater
number of key personnel to the new location than would be necessary
for a site nearer to our main factory. This could in turn cause
problems as it is felt that not many of our present staff would
wish to move to the Newcastle area on a permanent basis. Therefore
housing and cash incentives might prove necessary, which would add
to our costs....
... The large international port would reduce transportation costs
of shipping Swedish steel, because of its location. The cost of
transporting computer parts would rise but, as these are less
expensive, the increase should not be all that significant....
... The biggest problem with this location would be its relation
to the proposed new export markets of America and the Far East.
Situated as it is in the north-east of England it would increase
transportation costs to both export areas. This increase might well
be offset by the cheapness of the location in other respects....

13

Colourful club

AIM

To develop your skills in
- planning
- organising information

Introduction

The Penfield Youth Club, of which you are a committee member, has acquired new accommodation, but the whole of the interior is in poor condition and needs redecorating. The club can only afford to spend £100, so it has been decided that members of the committee will do the redecorating themselves. A scale plan of the premises is contained in Figure 1.

Task 1

Before the committee meeting to discuss the redecorating of the youth club, each committee member has been asked to draw up a brief informal report about his or her own proposals and plans for redecorating the club. This should include a brief description of the necessary materials and their estimated cost. In your report you should also indicate which factors you have considered to be of importance when outlining your scheme. For example, have you considered cost, or colour scheme, or hard-wearing materials to be the most important factor?

You can only exceed the £100 budget if you can suggest to the committee practical ways of raising the extra money.

Task 2

The committee meets to decide on the scheme to adopt for redecorating the club. Each member should be given the opportunity to outline his or her scheme. Remember that you will need to choose a chairperson.

To arrive at the best overall scheme, you might find it profitable to combine elements from different proposed schemes.

IMPORTANT

Read these information pages:
A Committee meetings
B Report writing

Figure 1   Architect's plans

Scale plan of Penfield Youth Club

All interior walls are 2.5 metres high. All doors are solid and measure 2 metres × 1 metre. All windows are of picture type, and all measure 1 metre in depth, except the toilet windows which are 0.5 metres in depth. There are no skirting boards. All walls are of brick-and-plaster construction.

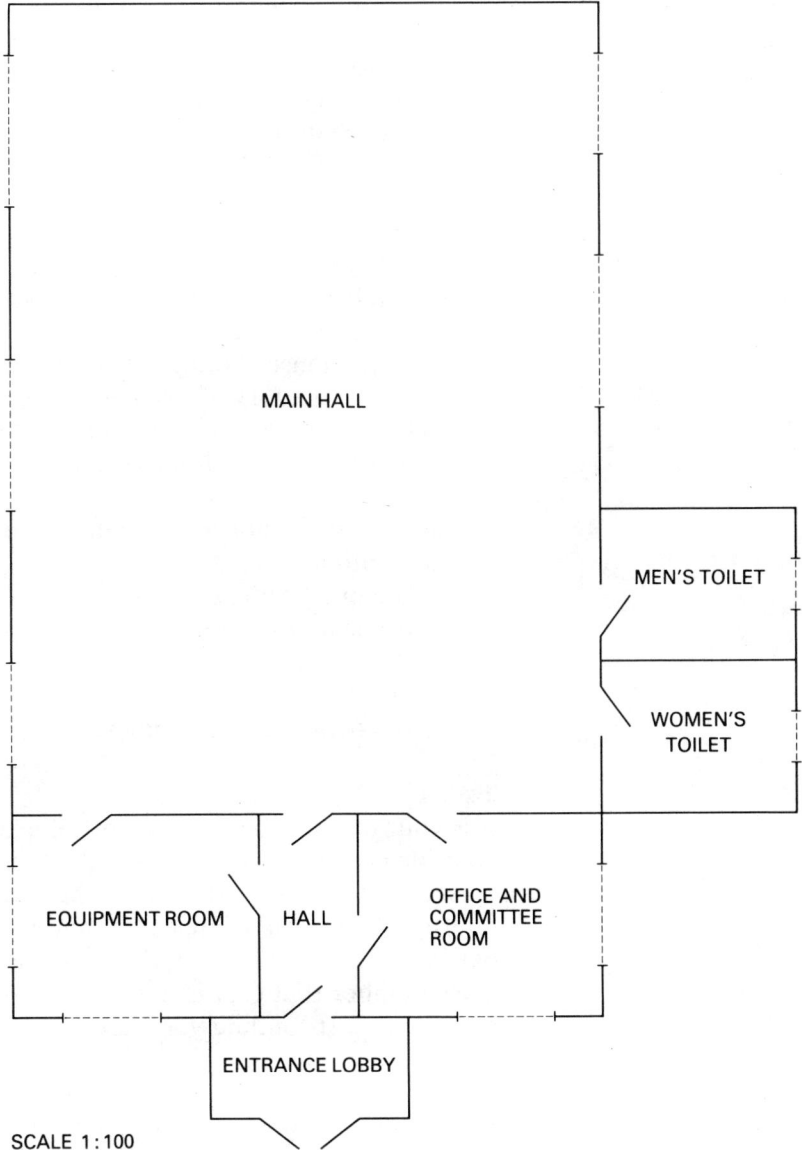

MAIN HALL

MEN'S TOILET

WOMEN'S TOILET

EQUIPMENT ROOM   HALL   OFFICE AND COMMITTEE ROOM

ENTRANCE LOBBY

SCALE 1:100

14 Redevelopment

AIM

To develop your oral and written skills in
- planning
- decision making

Introduction

A local businessman has acquired an old Victorian house (see Figures 1 and 2), standing in its own grounds. He has approached your firm about the idea of converting it into two self-contained flats.

Your firm is one of those chosen to propose designs for the conversion. The owner has stipulated:

(a) that each design should provide accommodation for two groups of residents from the following categories:
  - retired people – a flat for either a single person or a married couple;
  - a single-parent family – with no more than two children; and
  - single young people – aged between sixteen and twenty-five years;

(b) that the house should not be occupied exclusively by members of any one category of resident;

(c) that designs should not alter the external appearance of the house;

(d) that designs should not take the cost of conversion into account; and

(e) that the final choice of design will be left to a committee, which will take into account:
  - the practicality of the design;
  - the inventiveness of the use of space; and
  - the imaginative combination of resident groups, putting emphasis on the contribution each resident group could make to the daily life of the other.

Task 1

It is your task to draw up a report, illustrated with diagrams, outlining your ideas for the conversion of the house.

Assume that the exterior of the house is sound and restrict any internal structural changes to minor ones – for example, simple partitions or relocating doors and windows.

Remember that cost is unimportant at this stage, but it is essential that the reports outline your designs without giving too much detail.

Task 2

Working in groups, you now have to take the role of the committee that will choose the best design. Each member should present his or her report to the committee, and describe briefly to other members why that design was chosen and why it is worth the committee's consideration. Remember that your committee should take into account the points made in the introduction to this assignment.

By the end of the meeting the committee must have chosen the one design that they can recommend to the owner.

Task 3

Using the design that the committee has chosen, you have been asked to draft an advertisement to be placed, at a future date, in the local paper. This will give details of the scheme and will invite prospective residents to apply for a flat at the new site.

The advertisement can be drafted on one sheet of A4 and should clearly stipulate any conditions of residence.

____**IMPORTANT**____

Read these information pages:
A Committee meetings
B Report writing

Figure 1   Extracts from an estate agent's description

A pleasant, Victorian residence, situated in its own grounds, in a quiet residential area and only five minutes' walk from the new shopping centre. The exterior has been extensively renovated recently.

INTERIOR DETAILS - GROUND FLOOR

Lobby:	3m x 3m.
Hall:	3m x 12½m.
Lounge:	6m x 9m, with two fireplaces (containing gas fires), TV aerial point, and telephone socket.
Cloakroom:	1½m x 3½m, with old-fashioned WC and wash hand basin.
Kitchen:	5m x 3½m, with plumbing for hot and cold water, and gas-cooker connection.
Dining Room:	6½m x 5m.

INTERIOR DETAILS - FIRST FLOOR

Landing:	3m x 9½m, with telephone socket.
Bedroom 1:	9m x 6m, with fireplace (containing a gas fire) and TV point.
Bedroom 2:	6m x 3m.
Bedroom 3:	6½m x 5m.
Dressing Room:	3½m x 3m.
WC:	1½m x 3½m, with old-fashioned high flush toilet.
Bathroom:	2m x 3½m, with bath and wash hand basin in cast iron.

Figure 2   Architect's plans

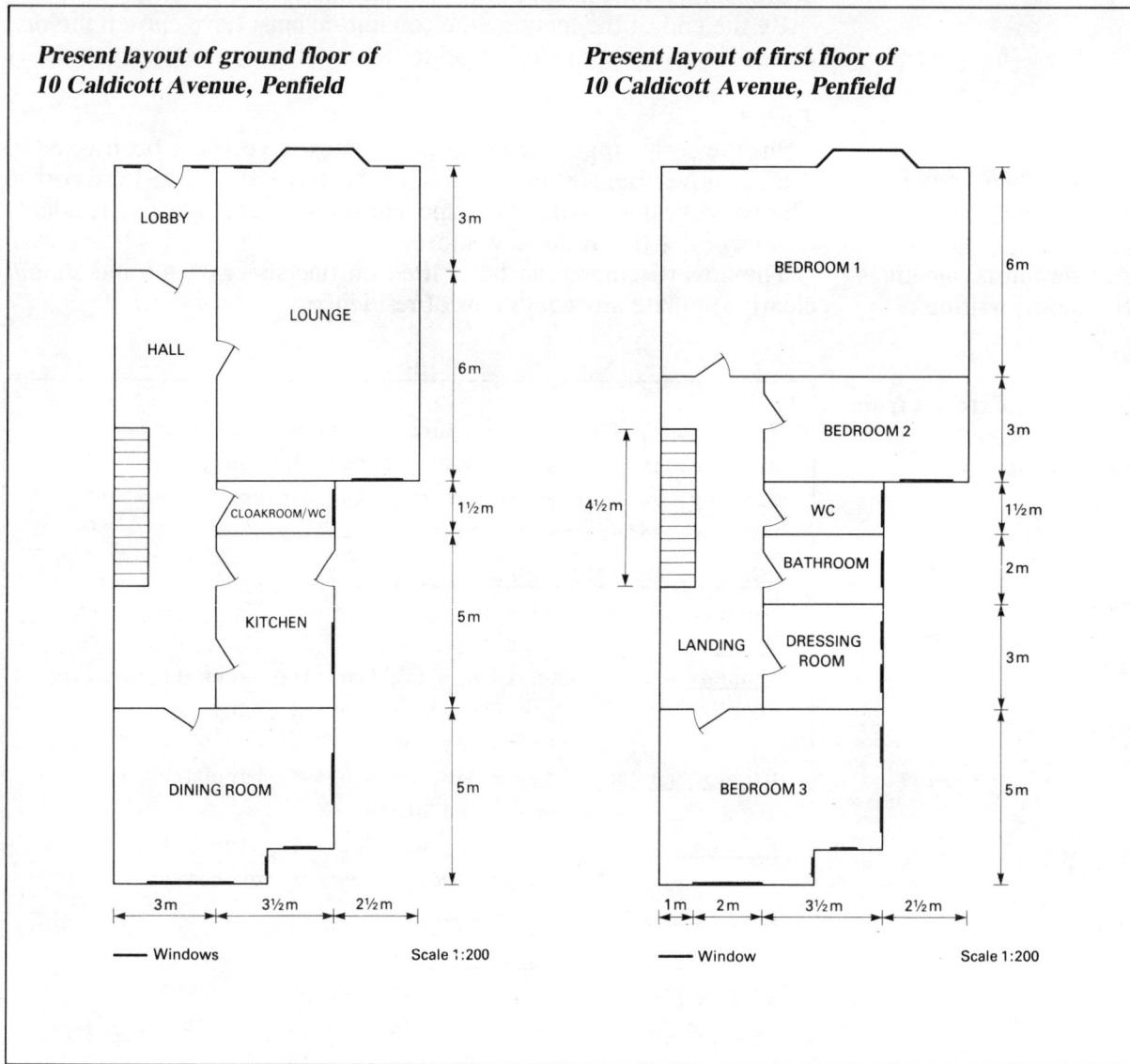

*Present layout of ground floor of
10 Caldicott Avenue, Penfield*

LOBBY

LOUNGE

HALL

CLOAKROOM/WC

KITCHEN

DINING ROOM

3m

6m

1½m

5m

5m

3m   3½m   2½m

— Windows   Scale 1:200

*Present layout of first floor of
10 Caldicott Avenue, Penfield*

BEDROOM 1

BEDROOM 2

WC

BATHROOM

LANDING

DRESSING
ROOM

BEDROOM 3

4½m

6m

3m

1½m

2m

3m

5m

1m   2m   3½m   2½m

— Window   Scale 1:200

15

Treasure hunt

_____ **AIM** _____

To develop your skills in
- interpretation of
  visual information
- planning and
  organising orally

Introduction

You are a member of the Social Club Committee for a local firm and your Managing Director (see Figure 1) has informed you that the company is willing to sponsor a motor treasure hunt which will be open to members of the firm's social club. He wants you, as a member of the Social Club Committee, along with other Committee members, to organise this event.

Before starting the tasks, read Figure 1.

Task 1

The Committee has decided that before it meets to discuss the firm's proposal for a car treasure hunt, its members should gather some preliminary ideas about a route and possible clues. Your first task is to compile a set of notes about a possible route and suitable clues.

At a previous meeting it was decided that the hunt should be held on a Sunday afternoon, and, to allow for mishaps and problems, that the route should not be more than fifty miles in length. Also there should not be more than ten clues.

In order to complete this task you will need to use a detailed map of your own local area.

Task 2

In this task the Social Club Committee will meet to finalise the treasure-hunt plans. The Committee has the following agenda to work through:

(a) Apologies for absence
(b) Minutes of last meeting
(c) Matters arising
(d) Route of the treasure hunt
(e) Clues for the treasure hunt
(f) Rules for the treasure hunt
(g) Date of the treasure hunt
(h) Publicity for the treasure hunt
(i) Any other business
(j) Date, time and place of next meeting

When dealing with this task committee members should concentrate on items (d)–(h) of the agenda.

___IMPORTANT___
Read these information pages:
A Committee meetings
B Report writing
F Note making
You will also require a detailed map of the area in which you live.

Task 3
The committee has asked you to produce a written report for the Managing Director about the forthcoming treasure hunt. This report should be set out informally, and should include such information as:
(a) details of the route;
(b) a list of the clues;
(c) any rules; and
(d) the date of the proposed event and any other information that you feel would be of interest.

Figure 1 Memorandum from the Managing Director

HUNTER ENGINEERING

MEMORANDUM

To: Members of the Social Club Committee   **Date:** 16th May 86

From: Mr. H. Hunter, Managing Director   **Ref:** HH/JB

Subject: Annual Treasure Hunt

At a recent Board Meeting it was decided that the firm should do more to encourage employee participation in the firm's Social Club. To this end it was decided that an annual car treasure hunt should be organised. The company will supply £25, £15 and £5 for the first, second and third prizes respectively.

I have been asked by the Board to request that members of the Social Club Committee should organise this annual event and your co-operation and support in this matter would be appreciated.

It was felt that, as the aim is to encourage membership and participation in the firm's social event, only club members and their immediate families should be allowed to participate.

I hope to receive details of your proposals for this event as soon as possible.

Harry M Hunter.

---

16 Motoring choice

AIM
To develop your skills in
- planning
- decision making
- presenting information orally

Introduction
You work in the Transport Division of a large engineering firm as one of the supervisors. The Manager of the Transport Section has recently received a memorandum from the Transport Director about the purchase of new vehicles for directors, managers and sales representatives (see Figure 1).

Vauxhall Astra L estate car

Vauxhall Cavalier L estate car

Task 1
Your first task is to write the report requested in the Manager's memorandum (see Figure 1). This is a formal request, so your report should be laid out in a formal manner.

Task 2
The Manager calls together the supervisors who have drawn up reports so that they can discuss the final choice of vehicles for possible purchase. The Manager will ask each supervisor to summarise briefly his or her choice of vehicles, together with the reasons for purchasing them. The final decision about the choice of vehicles will be the Manager's.
Note   If the group taking part in this assignment is small, then the role

___**IMPORTANT**___

Read these information pages:

A Committee meetings
B Report writing
I Circular letters

You will also need to have access to various motoring journals, copies of *WHICH motoring* report and car manufacturers' catalogues.

of the Manager can be taken by the tutor. If the group is large and has to be sub-divided, then one member from each of the small groups should take on the role of Manager. The people taking on the role of Manager should also swap the reports which they have written for Task 1. They should then have the opportunity to put forward their choice of vehicles, each using the other student's report.

Task 3

The Manager has decided on his choice of vehicles and has given you the task of preparing a circular letter to be sent to all Sales Representatives, outlining the choice of vehicle and its general specification, together with any positive features it possesses.

Figure 1   Memorandum to Transport Supervisors

MEMORANDUM
EDGLEY ENGINEERING PLC

To: All Transport Supervisors   **Date:** 19th June 1986

From: Mr. A. Harding, Transport Manager   **Ref:** AH/JH

Subject: NEW COMPANY VEHICLES

    I have received a memo from the Transport Director concerning the purchase of a new fleet of vehicles. At a recent Board Meeting it was decided to end our present policy of leasing vehicles and to consider the purchase of our own fleet.

    In this connection I have been asked to draw up a list of proposed vehicles. To help me with this I am requesting that you draw up a report outlining which vehicles you would recommend purchasing and why. The terms of reference are these:

(a) There will be vehicles for three groups of employee:
    * company directors;
    * section managers; and
    * sales representatives.

(b) All members of each category of employee will drive the same make and type of vehicle.

(c) When recommending vehicles you must take into account not only the company's image but also the cost. The following price limits must be kept to:
    * directors' vehicles must not exceed £12,000 retail price;
    * managers' vehicles must not exceed £8,000 retail price; and
    * sales representatives' vehicles must not exceed £6,000 retail price.

    Please let me have your report as soon as possible.

a. Harding.

17

Brookdale Old People's Home

___AIM___

To develop your skills in
- decision making
- · assessing the consequences of decisions

Introduction

The assignment revolves around the problem of selecting from a shortlist two residents to go into an old people's home.

Brookdale is a purpose-built home for forty old people. It was built in 1974 and is one of two such homes in the town of Penfield, which has a population of approximately 150 000. It is administered and run by local Social Services staff, and largely caters for permanent residents who are no longer able to live in the community. The home can also offer short-term care to five residents in any one week.

The home is situated in Penfield, close to the town centre, which has a modern, purpose-built indoor shopping centre, containing two supermarkets, a chemist, a DIY shop, a butcher, a restaurant and various other shops. A local GP Group Practice of six doctors takes care of the residents' day-to-day health needs, and if the residents have to go into hospital they are admitted to a large general hospital about six miles from Penfield. There is also a long-stay hospital for geriatric patients about four miles away, and if residents become unsuitable for the old people's home then they are admitted here on a permanent basis.

The home has thirty single rooms and six double rooms which are arranged on three floors. Each floor has a small lounge for residents and there is also a large lounge situated on the ground floor. A lift serves all floors. Toilet and bathing facilities are located on each floor. There is a communal dining room for residents, but some of the more able and mobile residents can make use of small kitchens, which are situated on each floor, for preparing light snacks or for making cups of tea or coffee.

The administrative office for the home is situated on the ground floor, along with the staff room and the residents' dining room.

The management team at the home is faced with the following potential problems:

(a) an ex-resident has left the home £3000 in his will and they have to decide how the money will be spent; and
(b) they have two vacancies for long-term residents so they have to decide, from a shortlist, who they will admit.

The social-work team is also faced with a potential problem: they have to decide who they will recommend to be admitted to the home.

Note You may wish to divide into two groups, a management team and a social-work team, depending on how you wish to complete this assignment.

Task 1 – Management team
It is your task, individually, to produce a written report on how you would like to spend the £3000 that has been left to the home. The report should outline your idea for using the money, how your chosen scheme will work, its advantages and how it will benefit the residents. Figure 2 contains an extract from the ex-resident's will and Figure 3 some suggestions for possible schemes which might benefit the home. However, these are only suggestions and you are free to make your own choices.

Task 1 – Social-work team
It is your task, individually, to produce a written report on the two old people who you feel should be admitted to the two vacancies which currently exist at Brookdale. Figure 1 contains information about six old people who are at the top of the waiting list for a place at the home.

The report should contain brief details about the two people selected, and should also contain valid reasons as to why these people rather than the others should be offered places.

Task 2 – Management team
For this task the team, as a group, must decide on the *one* scheme that they will adopt to spend the £3000. Each team member must be given the opportunity to outline his or her scheme and to indicate the reasons for their particular choice.

Task 2 – Social-work team
The social-work team should meet and, from their written reports, decide on which two residents they feel could be admitted to Brookdale. They should also draw up a list of reasons why they think the other candidates should *not* be selected by the management team.

Task 3 – Management team
Before beginning this task, re-read Figure 2, which contains an extract from the ex-resident's will. The will states that residents of Brookdale have to be informed of the management team's choice about how to spend the money and that the residents should also be given the opportunity to express their opinions about the decision.

The management team has given you the job of preparing a leaflet that explains the management's proposals for spending the money. The leaflet should:
(a) contain an outline of the team's proposal; and
(b) inform residents of the intention to hold a meeting to which all residents are invited and at which they will be free to express their opinion on the management's decision.

Your leaflet should include such basic information as date, time and place of the meeting.

___IMPORTANT___

Read these information
pages:
B Report writing
H Leaflets

Task 3 – Social-work team
Working in pairs, you have to perform a role-play informing one of the candidates on the shortlist that he or she has been unsuccessful in obtaining a place at Brookdale. One person should play the social worker and the other the elderly person. The social worker should attempt to answer any queries that the candidate may have about his or her non-admission to the home. This role-play can either be tape-recorded or put on video-tape.

Figure 1   People on the shortlist for a place at Brookdale

```
Candidate 1

Name:  Bessie Townsville.
Age:  79 years of age.
Marital Status:  Widow.
Current Situation:  Mrs Townsville has been widowed for the
    last six years but she has a son and daughter who are both
    married. Her daughter lives close by and visits her mother
    at least twice a week.

    Bessie suffers from Parkinson's Disease and has recently
    had a spell in hospital receiving treatment for this.

    She is finding it increasingly difficult to manage at
    home, even with her daughter's support, the services of a
    home help and meals-on-wheels. She refuses to attend a
    nearby day centre which could help to ease some of the
    problems.

    All in all she seems to have given up since her husband
    died and she says she wants to go into Brookdale to die.
    Her daughter also wants her to go into the home.


Candidate 2

Name:  Fred Jarvis.
Age:  72 years of age.
Marital Status:  Bachelor.
Current Situation:  Fred Jarvis used to be a road sweeper for
    the local council. He has never married and until a few
    years ago he was looked after by his mother who died at the
    age of 88. He now lives alone and cares for himself. He is
    currently in hospital because he has diabetes and has had
    his left leg amputated above the knee. All this has
    happened because Fred does not eat the right food and
    forgets about the doses of insulin that he needs regularly.

    The medical social worker feels that Fred would be better
```

off in an old people's home as he finds he is not able to look after himself. Fred has reluctantly agreed to her making an application for a place at Brookdale, but inwardly he feels very unsure about taking such a big step as he feels he is perhaps a bit young.

Candidate 3

Name: Alice Harmon.
Age: 83 years of age.
Marital Status: Spinster.
Current Situation: Alice Harmon used to be a school teacher and has lived in a council run, warden-serviced block of flats for the past five years. She is a very independent old lady.

Problems have arisen lately because Alice's doctor has diagnosed that she is suffering from senile dementia. Her memory is very poor and she suffers from incontinence. She keeps knocking on other resident's doors late at night and forgets where her own flat is. Her flat, too, is not as clean as it used to be, but unfortunately Alice refuses to accept the services of a home help. She does not have any relatives who are able to help her.

The warden of the block of flats is finding it increasingly difficult to cope with Alice and an application has been made on her behalf by her social worker for a place at Brookdale.

The one thing that really concerns Alice's social worker is that Alice forgets about the fact that she has agreed to this application being made on her behalf: sometimes she says she will go, at other times changes her mind.

Candidate 4

Name: Lise Brown.
Age: 90 years of age.
Marital Status: Spinster.
Current Situation: Lise was admitted to a long-stay geriatric ward about two years ago. She used to be a housekeeper for a local Roman Catholic priest who had allowed her to stay on as a paying guest after her retirement. But when her sight failed and she had several bad falls, she had to be admitted to hospital. As a result

of these falls Lise broke her hip, and this was very painful and slow to mend. Father Thomas has said that she cannot return to live with him in the house.

She has now made a better recovery than anyone ever thought she would, although she is practically blind. The medical social worker feels Lise could manage in an old people's home and has made an application to Brookdale on her behalf.

Lise has accepted this but secretly feels unhappy about having to get used to living somewhere else. The hospital would like Lise's bed for another elderly patient.

Candidate 5

Name: Bertha Bright.

Age: 88 years of age.

Marital Status: Widow.

Current Situation: Bertha has been a widow for about ten years and since the death of her husband, who was a bank manager, she has suffered from severe depression which has necessitated her admission to a mental hospital on at least three occasions.

The couple had no children and Bertha's friends feel that she would be better off in a home where she would have company. Bertha's GP also supports this viewpoint. She has plenty of money and could afford to pay to go into a private home, but Bertha's closest friend, Ann Holmes, is already a resident at Brookdale and she would prefer to go there.

She would have to pay the full charge if she were admitted there: this is now approximately £115 per week. Social Workers have agreed to an application being made to Brookdale on Bertha's behalf.

Candidate 6

Name: Mary Wigglesworth.

Age: 79 years of age.

Marital Status: Married.

Current Situation: Mary Wigglesworth suffered a stroke about six months ago, which left her partially paralysed down her left side. She can walk a little way with the aid of a zimmer but is largely confined to a wheelchair. Her husband

Sid is in remarkable health for his age but finds it hard
going looking after Mary, even though they have a home help
and the district nurse calls every morning to get Mary up.

Sid and Mary do not get on with one another as well as
they used to and Sid would like Mary to go into Brookdale
permanently, although their social worker feels it should
be only on a short-stay basis in order to give Sid a rest
occasionally. The couple live in a small, modern bungalow
which suits their needs quite well. They have a daughter
who lives close by and she is very supportive to the couple.

Mary knows that an application has been made to Brookdale
but feels that Sid is just trying to get rid of her, which
she feels very upset about.

The social worker feels that perhaps it would be better
if they were admitted together if a suitable vacancy arose.

Figure 2 Extract from an ex-resident's will

This is the last will and testament of me

ARCHIBALD ARBUTHNOT JONES of
Brookdale, Penfield . . .

4 I give the following legacies, free of duty . . .
(c) £3000 to be used on a project which will enhance the lives of all residents at Brookdale where I spent the last happy years of my life. I direct that executors or trustees shall be satisfied that residents of the home have been duly notified of the legacy and have been able to express their opinion, to the management, about how this money should be spent. . . .

Figure 3 Some suggestions for spending the legacy

Buying some garden furniture or a summer house for the garden
Buying continental quilts for each of the residents' beds
Opening a small shop for residents' use
Buying a new bath for handicapped residents
A holiday for residents
Equipping a bar and games room
Opening a small bar in the home for residents' use
Buying a video recorder for the main lounge
Equipping a room as a hairdressing salon
Investing the money and using proceeds to organise day trips for residents

18 Catering for Christmas

AIM

To develop your skills in
- organisation
- administration

Introduction

Catering students of Penfield College of Further Education have decided that it would be a good idea to organise a Christmas party for a group of old people from a nearby old people's home.

A committee of catering students has already been formed to organise the event and has raised the sum of £200.00. £100.00 of this has come from organising a raffle and £100.00 from Student Union funds.

The committee has written to the head of their department seeking permission for the use of the training restaurant for this function, and Figure 1 contains his reply.

The committee has also written to the officer in charge of Brookdale, the old people's home, suggesting that they would like to entertain some of the old people at a party and seeking general information about the kind of people likely to be attending the function. Figure 2 contains the reply.

Task 1

Each committee member has been asked to draw up an informal report, taking into account the reply from the officer in charge. This report should contain:
(a) the proposed date and time of the party;
(b) the proposed menu and the approximate overall cost; and
(c) possible activities to entertain the guests, and the cost of these, if any.

Task 2

In this task the committee should meet and discuss the various proposals drawn up for the forthcoming party. Each member should briefly summarise his or her own ideas for the benefit of other committee members. The committee can decide to adopt one person's ideas, or to adopt a combination of ideas from several people.

Task 3

The committee has given you the task of drafting a letter of invitation to be sent to each of the old people being invited to the party. This letter should contain the date and the time of the party, and a brief description of the menu and the kind of entertainment that is planned.

IMPORTANT

Read these information pages:
A Committee meetings
B Report writing
I Circular letters

Figure 1   Memorandum from Head of Catering Department

MEMORANDUM
PENFIELD COLLEGE OF FE

To: Catering Students' Committee   **Date:** 30 Oct. 1986

From: Mr. R. Day, Head of Catering Department   **Ref:** RD/TS

Subject: Proposed Christmas Party for Brookdale Residents

     Thank you for your memo dated 27th October asking whether you can use the training restaurant for one afternoon and evening towards the end of this term to hold a Christmas party for old people from Brookdale. I think this is an excellent idea. Congratulations!

     Unfortunately, because of other bookings for the restaurant at this time of year and the problems of ancillary staff working overtime, I will have to request that you hold the party on 3 December – all later dates are taken up with other departments using our facilities for their own Christmas celebrations.

     I do hope this date is convenient and if I can be of any further help please do not hesitate to ask me.

R Day

Figure 2   Reply from the Officer in Charge at Brookdale

7 November 1986

The Catering Committee
Penfield College of Further Education
Monks Way
Penfield PF19 3BV

Dear Students

CHRISTMAS PARTY FOR RESIDENTS OF BROOKDALE

     On behalf of the residents at Brookdale I would like to thank you for your letter dated 30 October 1986, inviting them to attend a Christmas party on a date which is to be fixed.

Through our residents' association I have notified the residents about the party and approximately 38 have said that they would like to attend. Please bear in mind that these numbers are approximate, as winter is the season for colds and flu, and our elderly residents are very vulnerable. I do hope this will not make things too difficult for you.

Of the 38 residents who hope to attend the party there are four people who are diabetics and they will need special diets. I hope you can cope with this. Also two of the residents will be in wheelchairs and they will need special help on the day of the party.

I assume that you will let us have more details of the party as soon as possible. We have our own minibus so we would be prepared to bring the quests along in relays.

Once again thankyou for your kind invitation and we look forward to hearing further from you.

Yours sincerely,

Judith Simpson

JUDITH SIMPSON
OFFICER IN CHARGE

19   Charity can be profitable

AIM
To develop your skills in
- planning
- organising

Introduction

You and a group of friends in Penfield have decided that it would be a good idea to set up a stall and sell various items for charity. Some of your friends who are interested in the idea of setting up this stall already have several other time-consuming commitments so it has been decided that this experiment will be tried first at Penfield College for a trial period of three months. Then, if it is successful, you will try out the same idea in the wider community.

Setting up the charity stall will be like setting up any other small enterprise in that if it is to make a profit, a considerable amount of thought and planning needs to go into it.

Task 1

Before anything else can be decided, it is necessary to find out what sort of products it would be most profitable to sell on your stall. The group has therefore decided to carry out a simple survey among potential customers to discover the most popular and saleable items. Your first task is to conduct this simple survey and to analyse the results.

Task 2

Using the results from your survey, as a group, plan how you will go about setting up the proposed stall. An agenda, which is set out below, has been drawn up for the meeting. The group needs to discuss each item thoroughly, formulating a proposal for it.

Agenda

(a) What products should the stall sell?

(b) Should the products mentioned in (a) be purchased wholesale or would it prove easier and more profitable to make them ourselves?

(c) A possible site for the stall. (Use the layout of your own establishment for this task.)

(d) When will the stall be open for business and what will be the rota for manning it?

(e) The weekly expenses that will be involved in running the stall, including any rent to the college for setting up the stall.

(f) Sources for initial capital for stock. Where will this money come from?

(g) Which charity or charities should the profits from the stall be donated to?

____**IMPORTANT**____

Read these information pages:
A Committee meetings
C Social-survey techniques
J Memoranda

Task 3

You have been asked by the group to write a memo to the Principal of Penfield College, outlining your ideas for the proposed charity stall and seeking his permission to carry out such an enterprise on college premises.

20 Selling spree

AIM

To develop your skills in
- planning
- presenting information orally
- decision making

Introduction

You work as one of the departmental staff at Dibbens Department Store in Penfield. Trade in some departments has been rather slack recently and because of this a new promotional campaign is about to be launched. This will involve all departments.

You have received a memorandum from your Head of Department outlining the format of the new campaign and how it will affect you. Figure 1 contains a copy of this memo. You should read all the figures before completing any of the tasks.

Task 1

The first task is for the group to decide, using Figure 2, which department in the store they would all like to be working in. All members of any one group must agree to be working in the same department. If it is a large group, then sub-groups can be formed representing different departments in the store. Figure 2 does not contain an exhaustive list of departments – if you wish to represent some departments not mentioned, you are free to do so.

Task 2

Your task here is to produce a set of notes, together with a diagram, that satisfies the requests made by your Head of Department in Figure 1.

The diagram can either be on plain paper or on an overhead transparency. The latter will make it easier for you to outline your ideas to the rest of the group when you come to Task 3.

Task 3

The Head of Department has called all departmental staff together to discuss, informally, the ideas that people have had for the window display and the advertising campaign.

You should be prepared to present your ideas orally to the rest of the group. The Head of Department will make the final decision about which scheme, or combination of schemes, to accept, but she should be open to suggestions.

If the group participating in this assignment is small then the role of Head of Department can be taken by the tutor. If the group is large and has to be sub-divided, then one member from another group should take the role of Head of Department.

_____IMPORTANT_____

Read these information
pages:
A Committee meetings
E Writing articles
F Note making
G Public speaking

Task 4

The Head has given each member of her Department a job to perform in
order to launch this campaign successfully. You have been given the
task of producing a five-hundred-word promotional article which will
appear in the local newspaper during the two weeks of your
Department's promotional campaign. Your article should consist of a
very brief history of the store, a list of what your Department sells and
what special promotions you are using during your campaign, and
details of any special goods, credit facilities or services available.

**Figure 1 Memorandum
from the Head of
Department to all staff**

MEMO

DIBBENS DEPARTMENT STORE

To: All Departmental Staff   **Date:** 26 June 1986

From: Ms J. Chand, Head of Department   **Ref:** JC/BS

Subject: Departmental promotional sales campaign

At a recent Heads of Department meeting the General
Manager reported that the Director of the store had decided
to take drastic measures to improve sales figures in most
departments.

The Directors have decided to combine a promotional
sales campaign with the introduction of a staff incentive
scheme. The scheme will involve the staff in helping to
organise and run, on a rota basis, departmental promotional
campaigns. Any extra profits from sales resulting from
these campaigns will be shared out among the departmental
staff on a percentage basis.

The Directors have also decided that Heads of
Departments should be responsible, with their staff, for
the organisation and running of the two-week campaign.
An advertising budget of £3000 per department has been set.
If the campaign proves successful, the amount to be spent
on advertising the promotion may be increased in the future.

I have decided that all members of staff should be
closely consulted and involved in this new scheme.
Therefore I would like each member of the department to
draw up a brief outline, in note form, of an advertising/
promotional campaign that the department could run on a
budget of £3000 lasting two weeks.

We have also been given window space that will be available for the fortnight of our campaign. It would be helpful if staff could provide a diagram outlining the sort of display that should be placed in this window. I do not need detailed drawings but outlines of where objects and material should be placed and an indication of the colour scheme involved. The window available to us will be the front window, to the left of the main entrance, which overlooks the High Street. The window measures 20 metres by 5 metres and the depth of the staging on which the display will be mounted is 2 metres.

Could members of staff have their proposals for the campaign ready as soon as possible, please, as I intend to call a meeting to discuss and decide upon our team's ideas and approach for the campaign?

The campaign not only gives us the chance of earning more money for ourselves – it also gives us a very good opportunity to show the Board of Directors and other departments what members of this Department can achieve – SO GO TO IT!

J E Chand

Figure 2 List of departments

G	Beauty, Hairdressing and Toiletries
3	China, Glass and Tableware
3	Customers' Cafeteria
LG	DIY and Decorating
LG	Electrical Appliances
1	Footwear
3	Furniture, Soft Furnishings and Carpets
G	Jewellery
1	Ladies' and Girls' Wear
2	Men's and Boys' Wear
2	Motoring
2	Sports and Leisure Equipment
G	Stationery, Books, Records and Office Equipment
1	Toys and Babycare
LG	Travel Department
G	Young Generation Boutique

Figure 3 Extracts from an article in the *Penfield Telegraph* dated 29 November 1986

Changes at the Top

Dibbens Department Store announced, yesterday, that changes were to be made at the top of their management structure.

The Company stated that Mr Steven Dibben, aged fifty-nine, will be retiring as Managing Director at the end of the year, but he will still remain on the Board in a non-executive capacity. The Company also announced that the present General Manager, Mr Gordon White, aged fifty, will also be retiring through ill health and his job will be taken over by Mr Martin Bashir, aged thirty-nine, who is at present the Manager of the DIY and Decorating section at the store. . . .

. . . Dibbens has been associated with the town of Penfield for over eighty years. It was originally set up by Mr Arthur Dibben, the grandfather of the present Managing Director, in 1907, as a small haberdashery shop in the High Street. Over the years the small shop has gradually expanded to become the area's largest independent department store with sixteen separate departments. . . .

. . . A Company spokesman stated, yesterday, that the Board had decided on a successor to Mr Steven Dibben but it had been decided not to release the name of the new Managing Director at present. It was made clear that the person taking on the job would, for the first time in the store's history, be someone outside the Dibben family, who had vast experience in the retail trade and who would also continue the Dibbens tradition of reliability and service. . . .

. . . These changes at the top of Dibbens represent a dramatic and courageous attempt by Dibbens' Directors to counteract the recession that has hit most of the retail trade – a recession which has meant declining sales and stiffer competition in the High Street from the other nationally organised retail sales outlets. . . .

. . . There is little doubt that Dibbens has reached a turning point in its history. Not only is it appointing an 'outsider' to the Board, but this outsider is likely to bring with him or her a new, forceful, one might even say, revolutionary approach to management and selling! . . .

. . . We at the *Telegraph* wish Dibbens every success in its attempts to survive and expand. Penfield and its immediate area has a population in excess of 250 000 people and it is still growing, so there is undoubtedly room for a large independent store like Dibbens to succeed. . . .

Figure 4 Advertising costs for local newspapers, television and radio

Penfield Telegraph – cost of advertisements

The *Penfield Telegraph* has an average daily circulation of 65 000 copies.

Columns (each column is 6 cm wide)	Depth of ad. in centimetres	Cost per day £
One column	3 cm (min.) For each extra 1 cm (up to 40 cm) add . . .	12.00 3.50 per cm
Two columns	3 cm (min.) For each extra 1 cm (up to 40 cm) add . . .	24.00 5.00 per cm
Three columns	9 cm (min.) For each extra 1 cm (up to 40 cm) add . . .	140.00 15.00 per cm

For special position in newspaper including front page or TV page, add 10% to all above prices.

The *Penfield Weekly Advertiser* – cost of advertisements

The *Penfield Weekly Advertiser* has an average weekly circulation of 30 000 and is distributed free of charge.

Columns (each column is 6 cm wide)	Depth of ad. in centimetres	Cost per day £
One column	3 cm (min.) For each extra 1 cm (up to 40 cm) add . . .	11.00 2.50 per cm
Two columns	3 cm (min.) For each extra 1 cm (up to 40 cm) add . . .	22.00 3.50 per cm
Three columns	9 cm (min.) For each extra 1 cm (up to 40 cm) add . . .	100.00 9.00 per cm

Pen Valley commercial TV – cost of still caption advertising*

The total population of the area covered by Pen Valley Commercial Television is two million.

	Cost in £ per transmission		
Length of ad.	Off-peak pre-1700 hours Mon–Sun Cost per showing	Peak 1700–2300 hours Mon–Sun Cost per showing	Off-peak post-2300 hours Mon–Sun Cost per showing
10 sec	90.00	450.00	90.00
20 sec	130.00	630.00	130.00
30 sec	190.00	950.00	190.00

* The initial cost of producing a caption advert with script is £175.00

SPECIAL OFFER!!!!! A 20-second still caption advertisement shown 3 times per night (once pre-1700, once between 1700 and 2300, and once post-2300) for the all-in price of £550.00!!!

Pen Valley Radio – advertising rates*

The total population of the area covered by Pen Valley Radio transmissions is 1.25 million.

	Cost in £ per transmission		
Length of ad.	Off-peak 1000–1600 Mon–Sun	Peak 0600–1000 and 1600–2000 Mon–Sun	Off-peak Post-2000 Mon–Sun
10 sec	70.00	150.00	70.00
20 sec	125.00	275.00	125.00
30 sec	185.00	400.00	185.00

* The initial cost of producing the script and tape for replay is £90.00 for the first ten seconds and £25.00 for each additional 10 seconds.

Information pages

Committee meetings

Uses

Committees and meetings in general are one of the most important methods of communication used in industry and commerce.

Meetings
Meetings range from the very formal to the informal.

Committees
Committees are also a common method of communication outside industry. In your social life you may find yourself serving as a member of a committee.

Usual format

Because committees vary in function, their styles and procedures vary also. This information page explains only those items common and important to all forms of committee, namely:
(a) Agendas
(b) Agenda papers
(c) Minutes
(d) Written minutes
(e) Minuting secretary
(f) Chairperson

Agenda
The agenda normally consists of a single sheet which is issued to committee members well in advance of the meeting. Its function is to brief members of the committee about what is to be discussed at the forthcoming meeting and on the order of topics.

For the more formal type of meeting the agenda has a standard form. The first three items are normally:
(a) Apologies for absence
(b) Minutes of last meeting
(c) Matters arising
Then follow the special items of business which vary depending on the type of meeting. The final items on the agenda are:

( ) Any other business
( ) Date of next meeting
   Whatever type of meeting is being held, some form of agenda is vital.

Agenda papers
These are any additional material supplied with the agenda to provide committee members with background information about items that will be discussed at the meeting.

Minutes
These are written notes that record the discussions and decisions made at the meeting. If the committee is a regular one then the minutes of the previous meeting are sent to committee members with the agenda for the next meeting.

Written minutes
These should be:
(a) brief, but give enough detail to enable anyone not present at the meeting to understand what was said and what decisions were made;
(b) factual;
(c) written in complete sentences;
(d) orderly, giving a logical account avoiding repetition of items; and
(e) written in the past tense, using the conventions of reported speech.

Minuting secretary
The secretary has the functions of:
(a) making sure that all committee members have been notified, in advance, of a proposed meeting;
(b) ensuring that all committee members are supplied with all relevant material needed for the proposed meeting;
(c) dealing with correspondence relevant to the committee's work; and
(d) writing the minutes at the meetings.
   If you are new to minute-writing then it is a good idea to look at copies of past minutes. This not only gives you a good idea about what is required, but will also help you to keep a continuity of style, which is important if different 'minute writers' are working for the same committee.

Chairperson
The chairperson has the function of making sure that the

meeting achieves its intended aims and that everyone who wishes to speak has a chance to do so.

For a chairperson to be effective he or she needs to:

(a) preplan and establish what the aims of the meeting are;
(b) state clearly at the beginning the purpose of each item to be discussed;
(c) control the meeting throughout, without being domineering;
(d) prevent anyone hogging the discussion but also encourage non-speakers to participate;
(e) keep the discussion to the point;
(f) be able to sum up the discussion and decisions made by the committee; and
(g) make sure that a record of the meeting's discussion and decisions has been taken.

Advantages

(a) Committees can bring people with a variety of experience and expertise together for the mutual benefit of all.
(b) Committees can generate new ideas and can indicate possible reactions to proposed ones.
(c) Committees give an opportunity for minority views to be expressed and considered.

Disadvantages

(a) Committees take time to deal with issues because:
 • it is necessary to give prior notice of meetings; and
 • the members have either to arrive at a group majority decision or at least to listen to other points of view before implementing proposals.
(b) Unless committees are properly organised and conducted they can waste time, effort and money.
(c) Committees do not always function effectively because they rely heavily on the possession of good oral skills.

B   Report writing

Uses

Reports are used in organisations to inform people, at different levels, about policy decisions, research developments, technical changes and so on, which are taking place both inside and outside the organisation.

Reports appear in various formats and range from the simple, for example the report form, commonly used in industry to report accidents, to large and lengthy documents covering many pages, such as parliamentary reports.

A report is usually written in response to a request from people in authority, and is normally restricted by *terms of reference* which require the report writer to provide specific information or answers to issues or problems.

Usual format

As already mentioned, reports come in many differing formats, but there are certain common points:

(a) The language used is formal and usually in the third person.

(b) The style is objective and the writer is required to be as factual and as unbiased as possible in analysing information. Unless they are specifically asked for, personal opinions should not be given; and if they are, they should be limited to the 'conclusion' section.

(c) Headings are normally used, and points made in the report are numbered or lettered for greater clarity.

(d) As reports are usually written and produced for the benefit of people in authority, the language used must be clear, and free from any ambiguities.

Both informal and formal reports have the above characteristics in common, so that when writing any type of report these points must be kept in mind. Formal reports have one other important characteristic which is a formalised layout using prescribed headings.

Layout of formal reports

Title page

This should indicate the nature of the report, the date it was written, the name of the author, and the name of the person who asked for the report to be written. This information should be set out neatly and attractively and acts as the cover for the report.

Table of contents
This is only necessary if the report is a lengthy one.

Summary
This is written if the report is a long one. The summary provides a brief survey of the ground covered by the report and indicates whether the objective of writing the report was achieved or not. The summary enables people to grasp the main points being made by the report without having to read the whole report.

Introduction
This is used to outline the terms of reference that affect the report. The terms of reference indicate the limitations of the subject matter that is to be investigated and the report must confine itself to that subject matter. This means that the introduction is very important because it lays down the areas to be discussed in the body of the report.

Main body
The main body of the report considers in depth the issues identified in the introduction. This section also explains how information was gathered for the report. For example several members of staff may have been interviewed. In this section subdivisions with appropriate headings should be used.

Conclusion
This should summarise the discussion that has taken place in the main body of the report, including a summary of the important points.

Recommendations
These tell the reader how the problem or situation being analysed can best be solved in the view of the author of the report.

Appendices
These are a useful way of presenting detailed information which, if it was included in the body of the report, would disrupt the flow of the report. Appendices might consist of statistical data, tables and graphs which are not strictly related to the main argument being presented in the report, but which are of some interest to the reader.

Bibliography
A particularly lengthy report may need to include a bibliography – a list of books or magazines to which reference has been made in preparing the report. The bibliography, if there is one, is usually placed at the end of a report.

Advantages

(a) Reports are a good method of presenting factual data in a concise way.
(b) Short reports, such as accident reports, can be condensed into a short stereotyped form for quick and efficient use.
(c) As reports have a formal structure it is relatively easy for readers to find and analyse the information relevant to their needs.

Disadvantages

(a) If not well written and constructed, this form of written communication becomes tedious to the reader and difficult to follow.
(b) Reports are a very formal method of conveying information to a number of people, and some other method of communication may be better.

AA LEGAL SERVICES — ACCIDENT REPORT

AA Ref:

Members who wish to obtain advice or assistance in their claims against another party as a result of a road accident are requested to record all the available details on this form and return it with all documents (or copies of documents) concerning the accident.

To comply with the conditions of a motor insurance policy, the insured (or his legal personal representative) must give notice in writing to the insurers as soon as possible after the occurrence of any accident and/or loss and/or damage with full particulars. Please ensure that you comply with all conditions of your insurance policy. **Please use block capitals for names and addresses.**

	A—MEMBER DETAILS	**B—DRIVER DETAILS (if different from 'A')**
SURNAME	MR/MRS/MISS	MR/MRS/MISS
FORENAMES		
ADDRESS		
TELEPHONE No.	HOME BUSINESS	HOME BUSINESS
AGE AT TIME OF ACCIDENT		
OCCUPATION		

PARTICULARS OF MEMBER'S VEHICLE

MAKE AND MODEL:	REGISTRATION NO:
YEAR OF MANUFACTURE:	ENGINE CAPACITY:

MEMBER'S OWN INSURANCE PARTICULARS

NAME & ADDRESS OF INSURERS:
INSURANCE POLICY NO. OR INSURERS' CLAIM REFERENCE:

INSURANCE COVER: COMPREHENSIVE/THIRD PARTY/THIRD PARTY, FIRE & THEFT/ROAD TRAFFIC ACT LIABILITY ONLY
(DELETE THOSE NOT APPLICABLE)

IS THERE AN EXCESS CLAUSE? YES/NO	IF SO, FOR WHAT AMOUNT? £

IF POLICY COVER COMPREHENSIVE, ARE YOUR INSURERS DEALING WITH CLAIM FOR COST OF REPAIRS TO YOUR VEHICLE? YES/NO

ACCIDENT DETAILS

PLACE (ROAD NAMES, TOWN OR VILLAGE & COUNTY)	DATE OF ACCIDENT
	TIME AM/PM
	SPEED IMMEDIATELY PRIOR TO ACCIDENT MPH
ROAD AND WEATHER CONDITIONS	

WITNESSES

NAMES AND ADDRESSES OF PASSENGERS IN MEMBER'S VEHICLE

NAMES AND ADDRESSES OF INDEPENDENT WITNESSES

Social-survey techniques

Uses

Social surveys in the form of questionnaires and public-opinion interviews have become a common technique of gathering information both in industry and by social scientists.

Purposes

In industry and commerce, survey techniques are used to monitor customer reaction to, and opinion on, a wide variety of issues – for example the colour and shape of packaging or the effectiveness of a particular advertising campaign.

Kinds of survey

The most common forms of survey techniques used are:
(a) *promotional campaigns* – for example the distribution of products to a selected area in order to assess customer opinion, or the use of free samples for the same purpose;
(b) *questionnaires* – these are used for gathering more detailed information about peoples' reactions or opinions; and
(c) *interviews* – this survey technique is not common in industry or commerce, and is mainly used when detailed or selective information is sought.

In this information page we will concentrate on the use of questionnaires.

Usual format

The public-opinion questionnaire can be used for a variety of purposes such as the assessment of peoples' political views or social attitudes, as well as to discover product preferences.

The questionnaire consists of a series of structured questions designed to draw from the interviewee specific answers.

To achieve this structure in a questionnaire, it is necessary to follow a certain procedure. The procedure can be divided into six stages.

Stage 1: Survey design

(a) You must first decide what it is you wish to find out.
(b) Then you have to decide on the number and type (for example, the age, sex and occupation) of people who you

think will be able to supply the required information, or be representative of such groups.

(c) Next you must choose the wording and order of the questions. The main problems to watch out for at this stage are these.

- *Wording* It is possible with questionnaires to word a question in such a way that you get the answer you expected. For example the quesiton, 'Do you think the Government should go to war to defend the liberty and freedom of its subjects?' would probably draw from interviewees a positive response to going to war. Whereas a question such as 'Should the Government go to war on behalf of another country?' would probably draw the opposite reply.

- *Bias* This is reflected not only in the wording used, as in the example above, but also in the way questions are constructed. By quoting figures of authority in questions, the interviewer is probably introducing bias into that question. People tend to respect authority and would not normally wish to be seen in contradiction to it. For example, 'Would you agree with the opinion of the majority of doctors that smoking should be banned in public places?' (rather than 'Do you think smoking should be banned in public places?').

- *Ambiguity* It is important to avoid the use of questions that are vaguely worded and that can therefore be interpreted in more than one way. For example, 'Are you in favour of government policies that affect old people?' is ambiguous because a 'yes' answer could be given for two reasons. The interviewee could mean that he or she is in favour of active policies in general, even though he or she feels that the existing policies affect old people negatively. The answer would also be 'yes' if the interviewee felt such policies affected old people positively.

- *Selecting questions* Here it is important to decide on the nature of the response you are seeking. In questionnaires there are two main types of questions: *closed questions* restrict the answer that can be given to either a 'yes' or 'no' answer, or to placing a tick in the appropriate box; *open questions* allow interviewees to answer in their own words. Each type has advantages and disadvantages. On the whole, closed questions are much easier to analyse but much more difficult to construct. In most questionnaires a mixture of both types is used.

- *Personal questions* In a general questionnaire, try to avoid too many personal questions, as people do not like answering such questions. If you do need to ask them, try to keep them indirect (closed questions are best for this). For example:

'How old are you?'
please tick box:

☐ under 18

☐ 18 to 35

☐ 36 to 55

☐ over 56

- *Order of questions* When designing a questionnaire, try to group questions of a similar nature together. This not only makes the progression more logical when answering, but helps later at the analysis stage.

Stage 2: Sample survey

In order to assess the soundness of a questionnaire a sample survey is normally conducted. This entails trying out the questionnaire on a proportion of the total sample.

As your time will probably be limited, we suggest that you try your questionnaire out on a few fellow students to see if it contains any structural problems. If it does then you will need to make the necessary alterations before conducting your full-scale survey.

Stage 3: Conducting the survey

There are three basic ways in which a survey based on a questionnaire can be conducted:
(a) selecting a sample group of people and then sending them a questionnaire by post, asking for completion and return;
(b) stopping a selection of appropriate people in the street and asking them to fill in your questionnaire there and then;
(c) the same as (b), but with the interviewer asking the questions and writing the answers on the questionnaire form.

The type of procedure you use will depend on the sorts of questions you are asking; people do not liked to be asked too many personal questions in the street but they might answer if the questions are sent to them privately through the post.

Each method has its own advantages and disadvantages. The main problem with method (a) is that there is normally a very high non-response rate. This could mean that your survey becomes biased because only a selective group of people respond.

Stage 4: Classifying the information

Once the survey has been conducted, some analysis of the results is necessary. Before this analysis can take place, the answers to the questions have to be classified; in other words, you have to examine the replies you have received and categorise them under headings or titles. With closed questions this is easy because all you have to do is count up the number of ticks or 'yes/no' answers. Categorising can sometimes be made easy by using the actual question in the survey as the title for your classification.

Stage 5: Data analysis

Once you have classified your data it is then possible to analyse it – that is, you will be able to look at the results and see clearly the conclusions you can draw. What these conclusions will be depends largely on the type of questions asked and the people interviewed.

Stage 6: Presenting your results

It is important to present your conclusions clearly and logically. This can be done by the use of statistical data, by graphical presentation, or by presenting them verbally or in a written report. The choice of presentation will depend on:
(a) the type and nature of questionnaire; and
(b) the nature of the audience being informed of your results.

For information on the presentation of statistical data, see information page D.

Here is an example of a questionnaire on present and future UK energy resources.

This survey's aim is to discover the public's awareness of present and future UK Energy resources: to find out the public's attitudes and reactions to the energy crisis.

OCCUPATION: _____

SEX: ☐ Male   ☐ Female

AGE: ☐ 16–20 ☐ 31–40 ☐ 51–60
            ☐ 21–30 ☐ 41–50 ☐ 60+

---

1. Which form of energy do you think generates the greatest proportion of electricity into the National Grid?

☐ Gas   ☐ Nuclear

☐ Oil   ☐ HEP (Hydroelectric power)

☐ Coal   ☐ Others

2. Which of the following do you think consumes most energy in this country?

☐ Iron and steel industry   ☐ Domestic

☐ Industry (others)   ☐ Others

☐ Transportation

3. Are you in favour of nuclear energy production?

☐ YES   ☐ NO   ☐ UNDECIDED

4. Which of the following 'alternative' energy sources have you heard of?

☐ Wind   ☐ Geothermal

☐ Solar   ☐ Plants (eg Water-Hyacinth)

☐ Ocean Thermal Energy Conversion   ☐ Splitting hydrogen

☐ Tidal   ☐ Others _____

5. Which of the previous list do you consider would be the most realistic future alternative energy source for the UK?

_____

_____

_____

6. Do you consider that the following are vital to UK energy production?

Natural Gas	Coal	Oil
☐ YES	☐ YES	☐ YES
☐ NO	☐ NO	☐ NO
☐ UNDECIDED	☐ UNDECIDED	☐ UNDECIDED

7. Do you have central heating?   ☐ YES   ☐ NO

   If YES please tick one of the following
   ☐ Oil   ☐ Electricity
   ☐ Gas   ☐ Other _____
   ☐ Solid fuel   _____

8. Have you ever seriously considered the use of Solar Panels at home?

   ☐ YES   ☐ NO
   If YES, what did you eventually decide and why?

   _____
   _____
   _____

9. Do you consider that an energy conservation policy should be an
   important consideration of our Government?

   ☐ YES   ☐ NO   ☐ UNDECIDED

10. Have you taken any steps towards conservation in your own home?

    ☐ YES   ☐ NO
    If YES please tick which of the following

    ☐ Loft insulation   ☐ Draught-stripping
    ☐ Cavity wall insulation   ☐ System controls
    ☐ Hot water tank insulation ☐ Double-glazing
    ☐ Others _____
    _____

11. Did you receive a local government grant for any of the above?

    ☐ YES   ☐ NO

D Compiling and presenting statistics

Uses

Industrial and commercial organisations use statistics to assess such things as the performance of the workforce, or products and costs, or profits.

Outside industry, television, newspapers and politicians commonly use statistics to support or discredit social, political and economic arguments.

Usual format

This information page concentrates on the advantages and limitations of various types of statistical data. We hope that the information provided will enable you to choose the most appropriate method when presenting your own data.

The important thing to remember about any method of presentation of statistics is that it must be accurate and appropriate to the intended reader.

The type of presentation also depends on the type of data available. In the following examples, five types of statistical methods of presentation are illustrated (Figure 1). Each example uses the same data, to help illustrate the advantages and limitations of the differing methods.

Tables

Advantages
(a) Tables are accurate in that precise data is written down.
(b) Tables give the user a detailed record of results.

Disadvantages
(a) With complicated data, much time and space is needed to interpret the results.
(b) It is hard to distinguish general trends simply by looking at a table.
(c) Tables are not a very visual method of communication.

Common usage
(a) Tables are mainly used to display results of research and experiments.

Graphs

Advantages
(a) Graphs are a visual form of communication.
(b) They are better than most other methods of statistical presentation in showing trends over periods of time.

Disadvantages
(a) Graphs are not very satisfactory for giving accurate statistical data. They mainly indicate trends.
(b) Graphs can only be used for simple data. The use of graphs for the presentation of complex statistical data results in visual confusion, especially if the data are closely related or overlapping.

Common usage
(a) Graphs are mainly used for time/series data – data that has been accumulated over a period of time. Thus the horizontal axis of a graph often represents some period of time, such as days, months or years.

Bar charts, pie charts and pictograms

Advantages
(a) All three methods of presentation are highly visual in their format.
(b) Like graphs, these methods of presentation are very effective at indicating trends.
(c) Bar charts have the added advantage of being able to portray quite complex statistical data clearly.
(d) Pictograms have the added advantage of additional accuracy – each symbol can represent a numerical figure.

Disadvantages
(a) All three methods are limited in their portrayal of exact information. Even pictograms do not present a totally accurate view.
(b) Pie charts and pictograms are limited in the amount of information they can portray; and pie charts, like graphs, are not very effective in displaying small-scale data.

Common usage
(a) These three methods are commonly used in newspapers, in magazines and on television, to portray general statistical information: they combine visual effect with varying degrees of accuracy.

Figure 1 Different presentations of statistics

Figure 1a *Table*

Where students of Penfield College spent their holidays

	1976	1980	1984
Britain	908	978	1152
Europe	762	771	724
America	211	216	187
Far East	61	68	59
Africa	28	35	25
Elsewhere	20	28	33
Total	1990	2096	2180

Figure 1b *Graph*

Where students of Penfield College spent their holidays

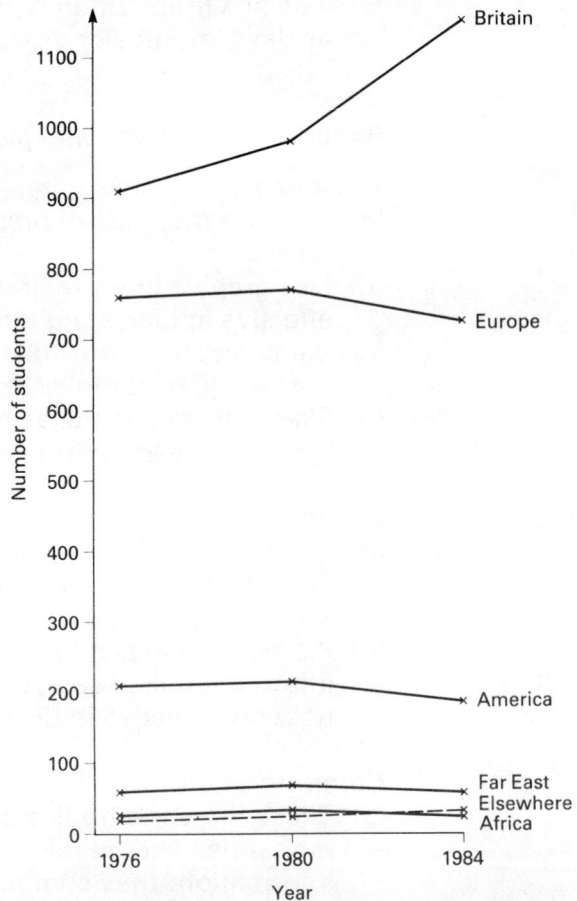

Figure 1c   *Bar chart*

Where students of Penfield College spent their holidays

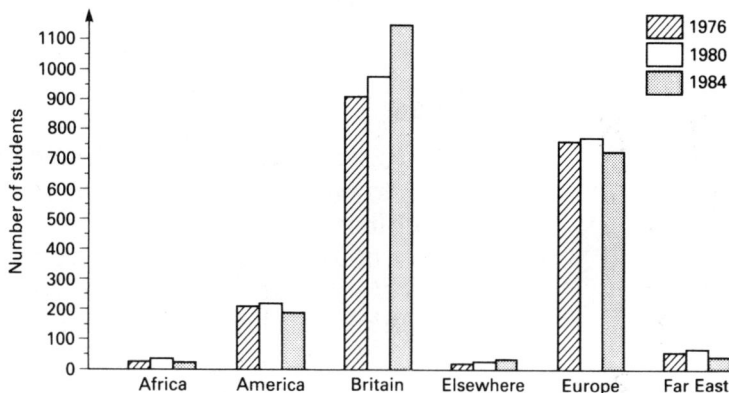

Figure 1d   *Pie chart*

Where students of Penfield College spent their holidays

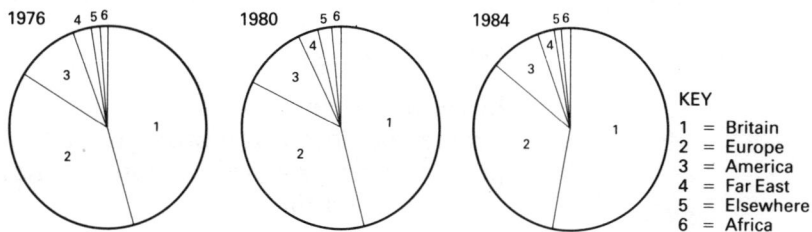

KEY

1 = Britain
2 = Europe
3 = America
4 = Far East
5 = Elsewhere
6 = Africa

Figure 1e   *Pictogram*

Where students of Penfield College spent their holidays

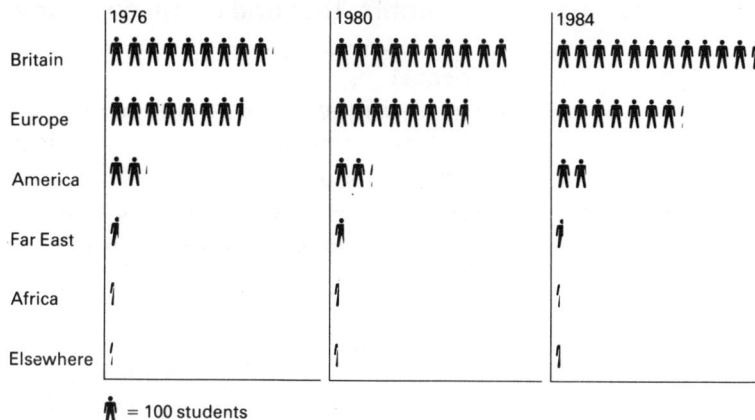

= 100 students

Writing articles

COLLEGE LIBRARY
COLLEGE OF TECHNOLOGY
CARNARVON ROAD
SOUTHEND-ON-SEA, ESSEX

Uses

People working in industry and commerce are sometimes called upon to write articles for local newspapers, company magazines or professional journals.

The nature of these articles varies, but broadly they fall into two categories:

(a) articles about some aspect of the company that the writers work for; or
(b) articles about some work expertise or specialism that the writers have, or about some trend to do with their particular area of work.

Usual format

Kinds of article

Articles fall into three broad types:

(a) *news articles*, which report on new developments within the firm or within a specialist field;
(b) *background articles*, which are mainly concerned with providing additional information, expert analysis or biographical and historical data about places or things; and
(c) *special-interest articles and features* – for example, an 'in-house' magazine may require an article on an unusual hobby that one of the company employees pursues.

Format

The format will vary depending on the type of the article and on the type of newspaper or magazine, but there are usually certain common features:

(a) the subject of the article will normally be prescribed, in advance, by the editor; and
(b) the article will normally be of a predetermined length.

Headlines

Sometimes an article writer is also asked to provide a headline for the article. Headlines are important as they attract the reader's attention and encourage him or her to read further.

Opening sentence
Likewise, the opening sentence of the article is also crucial because it, too, helps to persuade the reader to continue.

In articles, as in any other piece of written communication, the style and language used must be appropriate to the readership and purpose. For example, in a technical journal the language can be more technical than in an article on the same subject intended for general readership.

Advantages

(a) Articles in newspapers or company magazines are a way of presenting both the company's image and policies to the general public and to customers.
(b) Company magazines are commonly used to develop company loyalty and effectiveness amongst employees: they encourage personal involvement in the company.

Disadvantages

(a) Articles tend to be of use for general purposes. If one wishes to pass on important information to a clearly defined audience one cannot be sure that those needing to read it will do so.
(b) It is important that all articles are technically well written, with appropriate grammar and punctuation, and that they are stimulating and effective, otherwise they will fail to put over a positive company image.

F

Note making

Uses

The skill of note making is invaluable in a work setting and has many uses, for example:

(a) jotting down telephone messages;
(b) making appointments, dealing with complaints and taking orders or requests from customers or clients;
(c) making notes of instructions given by a superior;
(d) making notes about what is said at a meeting, or before speaking at a meeting, or prior to making a complicated telephone call;
(e) leaving notes for somebody else who is going to complete a job;
(f) summarising information, for example from a magazine or newspaper article, for a superior;
(g) planning a piece of written communication;
(h) planning travel itineraries or work programmes; and
(i) summarising information given in an oral report or lecture.

Usual format

Form

The most obvious characteristic of note making is that 'notes' are not written in sentences. Notes omit words like 'a' and 'the', and parts of verbs that are not essential to the meaning of the piece that the notes are about. Wording can be further reduced by:

(a) cutting away any words that are not essential to the meaning of the passage;
(b) altering the wording so as to convey the same sense but in fewer words; and
(c) cutting out any examples that are not essential to the meaning of the passage.

Skills involved

There is much more to note making than just using the minimum number of words. It relies heavily on the skill of *selection*, and when making notes you must be clear about the *purpose* of your notes. For example, if your brief is to find out about the advantages of vending machines, and you have a series of articles containing information about them, your notes should only reflect the advantages of these machines. Therefore remember:

(a) select only those items appropriate to your purpose; and

(b) keep the wording to an absolute minimum.

Abbreviations

The use of abbreviations in note making is desirable. Some common examples are:

(a) ref. = reference;

(b) C20 = twentieth century;

(c) shd = should; and

(d) info. = information.

There are many others. The main point is to make sure that you are able to understand your abbreviations when you come to read them at a later date. If someone else has to interpret your notes it is advisable not to use abbreviations other than standard ones. If you have to record names and addresses or unusual technical words in your notes, do not abbreviate them but write them out in full using capitals.

Arrangement of notes

Some notes will be brief and you will not need to worry about arranging the material. Others, summarising material from books, magazines, newspapers or lectures, may be quite lengthy and you will be faced with the question of organising the material.

Give the material a general heading: at a later stage this will help you to distinguish between essential and non-essential material.

If the material is from a book or similar source note:

(a) the title and author's name;

(b) the publisher;

(c) the date of publication;

(d) the number and title of chapter; and

(e) the page reference of any direct quotation, indicating any direct quotation by the use of quotation marks (such quotations should be kept to the minimum length).

Read thoroughly the material you are making notes on – you cannot make notes on anything you do not clearly understand.

When making notes of a general or lengthy nature, divide the material you are summarising into sections. For example break a magazine article into small sections; give each section a sub-heading before trying to make notes on it.

Number or letter your points under each sub-heading. This

will make for greater clarity when you refer to the notes at a later date.

Underline any points you consider to be really important.

Notes that are written whilst you are listening to someone speaking may present special difficulties. It is often hard to arrange the material successfully as you listen so you may well find it easier to make rough notes during a lecture and then restructure them as soon as possible afterwards. To help with this, it is useful to develop a diagrammatic approach to note making.

Advantages

(a) Well written notes jog the memory about tasks that have to be completed at a later date.
(b) Note making can save time. For example, well written and structured notes on a topic could save a great deal of time and effort in a work situation.
(c) Notes can be a useful aid to effective oral communication.
(d) They can save oral messages, such as telephone messages, from being forgotten.

Disadvantages

(a) Notes are ineffective if incomprehensible abbreviations are used, especially if the notes are to be used at a much later date.
(b) If they are written on scraps of paper, notes can easily be mislaid.
(c) If lengthy notes are badly organised, it may not be possible to follow them.
(d) Notes tend to be highly personalised which means that as a method of communication to others their uses are limited.

G Public speaking

Uses

Public speaking, which may include a speech, talk or lecture, is a formal verbal communication technique. It is used in a work setting to pass on information to groups of people – for example, by a supervisor giving technical instructions to a group of new apprentices, or a manager addressing people at a staff meeting.

It can also be used at formal social occasions – for example at a wedding reception or at a committee meeting of a club.

Usual format

Before starting

The format will depend on four points which should be considered carefully before beginning any preparation. They are:

(a) *The audience* This will affect not only the material included but also the language used.
(b) *The purpose of the talk* This will affect the material chosen as well as the tone.
(c) *The subject matter* Because most talks are limited by time, it will be necessary to select the data.
(d) *The presentation* Once the material has been collected, the speaker has to decide how to convey it to the audience.

Remember that these four points are all closely interrelated and that you should think carefully about them before any other preparation is attempted.

Preparation

Once you have thought about your subject matter and made a few notes under the four headings above, you should collect together relevant material.

The material can come from a variety of sources, including your own experiences, books, newspaper and magazine articles, film, television, and radio. Make notes from the various sources but keep in mind all the time the *purpose* of your talk.

You must now select and arrange the material that you have gathered. It must suit:
(a) the audience you are speaking to;
(b) the purpose of your talk; and
(c) the time allocated to your talk.
Remember that because of the last constraint you will be able to deal with important aspects only of a subject and not to cover every detail.

Planning the presentation
Once you have arranged the material you can now think about how you wish to present it.
   A talk is like an essay in that it should have:
(a) *an introduction*, which outlines the purpose of the topics you are going to discuss;
(b) *a main body*, which expands the topics already outlined; and
(c) *a summary or conclusion*, which summarises the main points of your talk and which may put over personal conclusions.
   You may wish to illustrate some aspects of your talk. Now is the point to consider where these illustrations will be placed. Remember that such illustrations must be simple, clear, and displayed in such a way that the whole audience can see them. Two examples are:
(a) presenting statistical data; and
(b) describing technical specifications, for example how a piece of machinery works.

Compiling the talk
Now it is necessary to begin compiling your talk. There is no set way to do this and it will vary from speaker to speaker. Some people like to write the whole talk out in full and then to condense it to note form onto small cards. Others write out the introduction and conclusion in full, leaving the rest in note form so that they can be sure of a firm start and finish.
   While you may wish to write out the talk in full, under no circumstances should you use this to give your talk. You will find the temptation to read it too strong, and reading word for word can be very boring for the listener and produces other distractions because you are not looking at your audience but at your paper. Also there is a considerable risk of losing your place, which causes unnecessary hesitation.
   A successful method is to put the main points and any factual data, such as dates and figures, on separate postcards. This

method enables you to keep eye-contact with your audience, and will also act as a prompt to help keep you on a logical progression through your talk.

Hints on presentation

It is natural to feel nervous when speaking in public. The best way to overcome this feeling is to be confident about your subject. That is why the preparation of your talk is the most important part.

Before you are called on to speak, make sure that you are familiar with the layout of the room and check that any equipment you might need is there and in working order. Also check in advance any notes and illustrations you wish to use.

Delivery

Delivery is important so remember the following points:

(a) speak clearly and audibly;

(b) speak naturally;

(c) speak to the whole audience and not just to one section;

(d) do not be afraid to use gestures and to put expression into your speech;

(e) do not speak too fast and do not be afraid to pause;

(f) if using a blackboard or illustrations, remember to face your audience whilst speaking;

(g) when using illustrations remember not to block your audience's view;

(h) try to avoid mannerisms such as jiggling things in your hands or playing with your hair, as this distracts and eventually irritates the audience; and

(i) speak slowly, giving the audience time to take in what you are saying or doing.

Questions

An important element of being a good public speaker is the ability to respond to questions from the audience. Normally a speaker invites questions at the end of the talk. If questioning takes place *during* the talk there is a danger of:

(a) disrupting the flow so that the audience forgets points already made;

(b) the speaker losing his or her place in notes;

(c) the speaker becoming sidetracked; or

(d) dialogue ensuing between questioner and speaker, thus neglecting the rest of the audience.

Remember that the acid test is not what you said but the *effect* of it upon your audience.

Advantages

(a) Public speaking is a method of conveying information to a large group relatively quickly and easily.
(b) A good and skilled speaker can sometimes have more impact than the written word.
(c) As it involves face-to-face contact, it allows the audience to show their feelings and responses.

Disadvantages

(a) Public speaking is not a good method of communication if it is necessary to pass on much detailed information.
(b) To be effective, public speaking relies heavily on the individual speaker's performance.
(c) Its effectiveness also relies heavily on such external factors as good acoustics, the availability of technical back-up and a responsive audience.

H   Leaflets

Uses

Leaflets are used
(a) to advertise products or services;
(b) to inform the public of their rights, entitlement to benefits, and public services;
(c) to inform people at work of possible legislation which might affect them (for example, health-and-safety matters, or information about income tax).

Usual format

Each leaflet comprises one sheet of paper. This sheet of paper can be folded in a variety of ways to present information in an interesting manner.

The style and content depends on the subject matter, but it is normally presented informally. Because of lack of space, information is often presented in note format, taking care to avoid misrepresentation of facts or ambiguities in the use of language.

Usually – to aid presentation – pictures, drawings, different-sized headings, and various colours are used.

Advantages

(a) Information can be presented to a wide audience quickly, cheaply and easily.
(b) Difficult and often complex information can be presented in a style that is easy to understand.

Disadvantages

(a) Because of a leaflet's size the information that can be transmitted is limited. It is therefore important to assess whether a leaflet is the most appropriate means of communication for the data concerned.
(b) Leaflets that are pushed through people's letter-boxes and distributed at random may need to rely heavily on the use of colour and 'punchy' language in order to make an impact.

(c) Complex issues, such as the pros and cons of pay claims, could be over-simplified by employing this method of presentation.

Additional material

A brochure employs the same techniques as a leaflet to achieve its intended aims, but it consists of several sheets of paper which are usually folded or fastened in some way. Brochures have the same uses in industry and commerce as leaflets.

Lone parents

One Parent benefit   CH.11

(non-contributory)

An addition to child benefit paid, regardless of income, to people bringing up a child alone. You get £4.25 a week for the first or only child.

Child's special allowance   NI.93

(National Insurance)

A weekly cash payment made to a woman whose marriage has been dissolved or annulled if, at the time of death of her former husband, he was (or should have been) helping to support one or more of her children. You get £7.65 a week for each child.

Tax allowances

Lone parents (widowed, divorced, separated or single) may be able to claim the 'additional personal allowance'. Together with your single person's allowance, which you get automatically, this will give you allowances equal to those of a married man. *Get leaflet IR.29 from a tax office or PAYE enquiry office.*

A widow may also get the widow's bereavement allowance, which is equal in amount to the additional personal allowance. This is given both in the tax year of bereavement from the date of bereavement to the end of the year and in the following tax year too. *Get leaflet IR.23 from a tax office or a PAYE enquiry office.*

Special conditions for benefits

Special conditions apply to lone parents applying for some social security benefits:

Family Income Supplement

You need work only 24 hours a week (instead of 30) to satisfy the 'full-time work' conditions *(see page 6).*

Supplementary benefit

Up to £4 of your earnings, PLUS half your earnings between £4 and £20, are not counted as income when you claim *(see page 5).*

14

Health benefits

People getting supplementary benefit, housing benefit supplement or FIS also automatically get free prescriptions, free glasses, free dental treatment, help with hospital fares, and free milk and vitamins for expectant and nursing mothers and children under 5. *See page 7.*

See leaflets

One Parent benefit	CH.11
Child's special allowance	NI.93
Help for one-parent families	FB.3

School or college

Free school meals

Children attending schools maintained by local education authorities, from families on supplementary benefit or FIS, are automatically entitled to free school meals, although you will usually have to claim them. But some education authorities also provide free school meals to other children. **If you want to know more,** ask at your local Education Welfare Office.

Free school milk

Some local education authorities provide free milk to all pupils up to 11, others for those up to 7. Some provide milk only to pupils in special schools, or who need it on medical grounds. In some areas, no free milk is provided. **If you want to know more,** ask at your local Education Welfare Office.

Fares to school

Children under 8 attending their nearest school and living more than two miles from it (three miles for older children), normally get free travel. Some education authorities give help even if you live inside these distances, or if your children attend other than the nearest school. **If you want to know more,** ask at your local Education Welfare Office.

15

Circular letters

Uses

Circular letters are used:
(a) to convey information to a large number of people – for example to tell employees in a company about a share-participation scheme for employees that is being introduced;
(b) to advertise and sell products and services to customers; and
(c) within organisations as an *internal* as well as an *external* form of communication.

Usual format

Circular letters are usually set out on headed notepaper employing normal letter layouts and conventions. The main difference is that circular letters often omit the recipient's name and address.

The salutation is important as it has to appeal to a wide audience – often the name of the person addressed is not known.

The use of subject headings and interesting opening paragraphs is vital when one is trying to appeal to a wide audience that has no particular prior interest in the subject matter.

A friendly, informal and persuasive tone may help to sell a product or service, or interest the reader in the information conveyed.

Presentation is also vitally important – a circular letter that is badly laid out and on poor quality paper will not interest anyone.

Circular letters try to appeal to people of all ages and personalities, so:
(a) language must be chosen carefully, avoiding use of jargon;
(b) important points must be presented in a logical order; and
(c) grammar and spelling must be accurate.

Advantages

(a) Information about a product or service can be passed on easily and quickly to a very large, varied audience.

(b) The sender has some degree of audience selection.
(c) Many companies use word processors and computers to send out 'individualised' circular letters.

Disadvantages

(a) No one can be certain that the circular will be read.
(b) Circular letters, because of their popularity among senders, can be annoying and over-persuasive.
(c) As circular letters have become a commonplace selling technique, their effectiveness is becoming less certain.

Here is an example of a circular letter.

PENFIELD HEATING SYSTEMS

60 Warner Road
PENFIELD PH1 6HN
Tel: 0892 476892

Date as postmark

Dear HOUSEHOLDER,

INSTALL NOW – PAY LATER

Don't have the shivers again this winter. Think about installing a new central heating system NOW – We have special offers which you can take advantage of this summer.

We are currently offering a special price on the installation of our oil-fired and gas central heating system, and if you decide to install a new system you need not make your first repayment until October. A typical example is given below:

        TO INSTALL A GAS CENTRAL HEATING SYSTEM
        IN A SEMI-DETACHED HOUSE, TO INCLUDE A NEW
        BOILER AND SEVEN RADIATORS, THE EXCEPTIONAL
        SUMMER PRICE OF   **** £950.00 ****

AND REMEMBER, WE CAN ALSO ARRANGE LOW COST FINANCE FOR YOU OVER TWO YEARS.

So ring us today on PENFIELD 476892 and let one of our representatives call and give you a quote for your new central heating system so you and your family will be WARM ALL OVER THIS WINTER.

Yours sincerely,

John Ryan

JOHN RYAN
Director, Penfield Heating Systems.

J   Memoranda

Uses

The memorandum is an *internal* form of communication, used for passing information between people and departments inside an organisation.

Usual format

Organisations, large and small, usually print or have printed their own stationery, so layouts may vary but they will contain the same basic information. Here is an example of a pre-printed layout of a memorandum (plural 'memoranda', abbreviation 'memo').

MEMORANDUM

PENFIELD ENGINEERING LTD

To: **Date:**

From: **Reference:**

Subject:

The name and position of the recipient appears at the top. Additional copies to other people may be listed at the bottom under the 'carbon copy' ('c.c.') heading. One copy goes to each of these people, with the recipient's name ticked off on that copy – this acts as a checklist, ensuring that everyone who is on the circulation list has been sent a copy.

The name and position of the sender appears below that of the recipient.

The date appears in the top right-hand corner, and may be abbreviated.

The reference appears immediately below the date.

A title summarising the contents of the memo appears in the 'SUBJECT' heading space.

Although 'memorandum' means 'a note to help the memory or record of events for future use', memoranda can run to more than one sheet of A4 paper, depending on the nature of the subject matter.

Memoranda are written in continuous prose, using paragraphs. If the subject matter is complicated, headings and numbered or lettered points may be used to simplify the material.

Memoranda may either be signed or simply initialled at the bottom.

Advantages

(a) A memorandum is a quick, simple and efficient form of *internal* communication.
(b) It can convey the required information to several people at once and can also keep other interested parties informed.
(c) It may not demand as much time as a letter.
(d) It provides a written record.

Disadvantages

(a) The information to be conveyed may be too long or complex for a memo. For example, an informal chat with a colleague or a quick internal telephone call may be more appropriate.
(b) Memoranda have to be filed: they can, and do, take up valuable filing space which could perhaps be used for more important documents.

Note

One of the variations you may come across in different organisations is the use of a colour-coded memorandum system. For example:
(a) white copy – author's copy;
(b) pink copy – for information only: no action required at the moment;
(c) blue copy – for action: the sender wishes the recipient to act on the information contained in the memorandum; and
(d) green copy – file copy for other departments (if needed).